Critique of Mainstream Austrian Economics

In the spirit of Carl Menger

'There is nothing more frightening than ignorance in action.'

GOETHE

CRITIQUE OF MAINSTREAM AUSTRIAN ECONOMICS

In the spirit of Carl Menger

An analysis of some aspects of the economics of

Ludwig von Mises

By ANTAL FEKETE

Based on lectures delivered at the

NEW AUSTRIAN SCHOOL OF ECONOMICS
(NASOE)

in Münich, Bavaria, Germany, September 2012

"Critique of Mainstream Austrian Economics"

by Antal E. Fekete, with a foreword by Peter. M. Van Coppenolle and editorial assistance of David van der Linden.

Also available in softcover (2019)
from the Pubisher ISBN 978-1097167937

Published independently
ISBN 978-90820655-27

Also Available from NASoE:

Credit And The Sources From Which It Springs: The Propensity To Save And The Propensity To Consume
Volume I (2019) ISBN 978-1093144260|ISBN 978-9082065534 (hardcover)
Volume II (2019) ISBN 978-1093203288 |ISBN 978-9082065541 (hardcover)
Volume III (2019) ISBN 978-1093220902|ISBN 978-9082065558 (hardcover)
Volume IV (2019) ISBN 978-1093254419|ISBN 978-9082065565 (hardcover)
The Austrian Business Cycle Revisited (2012) ISBN 5800094365307
Le Retour au Standard Or (French)(2015) ISBN 978-2914569897
Beyond Mises - Based On The Work Of Antal E. Fekete (2010)
ISBN 978-06153734-09 (Softcover)
Time of The Vulture (ISBN 978-0615677088)

Para libros españoles sobre economía austríaca : Amazon | Juan Ramón Rallo.

Online video resources that belong to the Money & Credit Series:
–https://www.youtube.com/channel/UCnz5gMwVp6VVTuxbHjZaB7Q
– https://www.youtube.com/watch?v=YN1vMdx-GiQ
Advanced Research Topics
– https://purelytheoreticalresearch.com
– https://www.juandemariana.org

Applied Investment Strategies by NASOE members
– https://bullionplay.com
– https://lbnow.co.nz
– https://drschoon.com
– https://monetary-metals.com
– https://goldstandardinstitute.us or .net
– https://survivethecrisis.com

Editor's Foreword 2016

This book is the result of a series of lectures given by Hungarian born mathematics professor Antal Fekete in Münich, Germany, during the summer of 2012 for students that attended his economics seminars. It contains the professors' theoretical critique of Ludwig von Mises. Both professor Fekete and von Mises belong to the same Viennese or Austrian school of economics. Von Mises was himself an Austrian by birth and had lived and worked in Vienna. Prof. Fekete fled Hungary just like von Mises had fled Austria a generation before, but for different foes. Von Mises feared for his life under the threat of the Nazi's, while Fekete narrowly escaped the Red Army's invasion of Hungary. Although prof. Fekete ended up in Canada as a mathematics professor, his preoccupation had always been the Viennese school of economics including Carl Menger, von Mises and von Hayek. The dispersion of the Viennese scholars with both world wars had brought about an unprecedented intellectual catastrophe and a tragic break up of the great philosophical traditions in Vienna. A few years later, European authorities no less underestimated the destruction and dispersion of intellectual capital, remnant in other territories previously grouped under the Habsburg Empire, under the hands of Soviet communist rule.

Professor Fekete sets out his non-destructive criticism of Ludwig von Mises, while having the greatest respect possible for von Mises' work and person. The points he formulates do not destroy, but rather complement the body of knowledge of Austrian economics. Nevertheless, criticism is never an easy endeavour, certainly not in the case of Ludwig von Mises. But let it also be clear from the start that professor Fekete only makes suggestions regarding pure economic theory and that his theoretical points are in no way to be interpreted as political stances, in the way the school of the American Austrians interprets itself sometimes.

Professor Fekete did not suddenly appear out of nowhere with this book – he too was inspired by predecessors, whom he had studied for all his life. Neither is this his first book or publication.[1] This book may be seen as part of a re-emerging interest in Austrian economic theory based on methodological individualism, seminally set out by Jena professor Gottlob Hufeland (1760 – 1817) and successfully improved upon with margin theory almost hundred years later by Viennese professor of political economy Carl Menger (1840 – 1921).

Carl Menger, mostly remembered together with Stanley Jevons and Léon Walras for the discovery of marginalism, deserves more accolade though. Besides being a professor of economics in Vienna, one of the most prestigious universities in the world, he became tutor of the Crown prince, Archduke Rudolph of the Austro-Hungarian Empire, not without merit, and served as president of many national scientific Academies. He was well respected throughout Europe and was appointed, amongst others things, as liaison officer for the French "Institut des sciences morales et politiques." To be sure, his version of marginalism in no way resembles that of Jevons, Walras or Gossen.[2]

Novices to the domain of pure economics may relax. There are no mathematical equations in this book to keep the brain sharp. But an introduction to financial algebra could not hurt either. In fact, understanding Fekete crucially hinges on grasping the basics of actuarial maths, usually an under-graduate subject in itself.

Throughout Fekete's writings, the overriding theme is pure theoretical research, free from ideology. An ideology is a set of beliefs and expressions that present and interpret the world in a way designed to organise and justify social and political action.[3] But what is "scientific" for today's modern scientists cannot be metaphysical otherwise it becomes a pseudoscience or an "ideology". (By contrast, truth never demands *justification*... nor any action.)

For professor Fekete however, what is "scientific" must not be dissociated from metaphysics at the risk of becoming an "ideology"... This position on ideology and metaphysics follows from Plato and Aristotle who risked their lives some 25 centuries ago, educating

Greek aristocrats by teaching the difference between a love of wisdom (*philosophy*) and a love of opinion (*philodoxy*). Both terms were Plato's; the former survived in the person of a philosopher, the latter is better known as an *intellectual*.[4] This focus on pure theory –averse of ideology– results in a complete and no doubt surprising reappraisal of the venerable but disparaged gold standard, its crucial role in setting interest rates and all its under appreciated benefits. Even more: a thorough knowledge of the gold coin standard, such as experienced by Menger who lived during the reign of the Latin Monetary Union, and who left no doubts about his position in his book on The Origin of Money (*Geld*)[5] is pivotal in understanding the issues at hand. Some of Mengers' so-called intellectual heirs missed certain aspects of the gold standard and in some cases even the entire point. In some sense, the advocacy of a thorough knowledge of the unadulterated circulating gold coin standard (cum real bills) as experienced by the world before World War I, will certainly be a political statement, especially if that knowledge is to become common sense knowledge (again), although this work has only a theoretical economic education as its aim. Let me remind the reader that the word "political" means, as it always has done since Hellenic times, "concerning the polis or society." (Greek philosophers thought and were concerned about the right order of their society or communities, hence the word political meant for them something less tainted then whatever it means for a lot of us.) Modern perversions notwithstanding and the economic survival of a civilisation being at stake, let there be no modernist hijacking of the meaning of this ancient, abused word. In fact this book reveals why the gold coin standard is a thorn in the eye of those you suspect the least. The gold coin standard - and its corollary the gold bill market, engender a most positive message for society in so far that it heralds a solution out of an economic impasse. The gold coin standard was surreptitiously "killed" in the same way Nietzsche declared us all murderers of God. The reader is reminded that the gold standard would exclude the need for central banking in its issuance function. The latter did not even exist before the Bank of England (1694) and consequently we most certainly can continue life without central banking, for it is only a blip in the history of mankind. That is the hope the gold standard entails, loose talk to the contrary will not do away with this historical fact. That the efforts to revive the gold standard after the war came to naught, should be sought in the Ricardian precepts of the gold *bullion* standard that was deployed disingenuously instead of the circulating gold *coin* standard.

With this the reader has been given a fair warning: any detraction from a gold coin standard may be inspired by ignorance at best or ideology at worst, usually a combination. The mark of a scientist is that he or she will always keep an open mind for arguments for or against; proper arguments, that is, not ignorant propaganda. Antal Fekete will try to cure ignorance. Against ideology I am not aware of the existence of a medicine, short of an exorcism.

Belgium, December 2016
Peter Van Coppenolle

Foreword 2012

I have always been an admirer of Ludwig von Mises (1881 – 1973) and long considered him the greatest economist of the 20th century. He was also a charming and a modest person. He would have never considered himself infallible. And he wasn't. After a long study, soul-searching and hesitation I called attention to points where in my opinion von Mises was wrong. With a great deal of diffidence and humility I am doing my best to defend my position vis-a-vis that of von Mises.

Accentuating the negative

I have always felt that the theory of gold money, as presented by von Mises and even more so by von Hayek, is a 'negative theory'. Friedrich A. von Hayek almost goes as far as saying that the gold standard is a necessary evil; there would be no need for it if the government could be trusted. According to von Mises it is the temptation to tamper with the value of the monetary unit that has made the gold standard indispensable.[6] In this way growth in the stock of money is tied to the profitability of gold mining. Von Mises thought it was necessary to add that "the gold standard is not a perfect institution: there is no such thing as perfection in human affairs." His position is motivated by the Quantity Theory of Money. Consequently he fails to distinguish between the value and the purchasing power of gold which, from the point of view of Menger, are two different concepts.

Positive theory of gold

In my view there is no need to be apologetic about the gold standard. Rather, there is need for what I call – in want of a better word – a 'positive theory' of gold.[7] I offer such a positive theory, and my main criticism of von Mises, von Hayek, and many other great economic thinkers going all the way back to Ricardo, centres around the fact that they have all missed the point of *contact between gold and interest*. More specifically they have missed the point of contact between gold and the 'curse of ageing'. Man's surplus of mental and physical powers will one day give way to deficit and he knows it. He prepares for the day when he has to draw on his savings. That is, provided that he has any: if central planners and central bankers have not embezzled it.[8] In fact, von Mises unfairly ridiculed John Fullarton by calling his reference to gold hoarding in reaction to the suppression of the rate of interest *"Deus ex machina"*.[9]

In the view of most economists gold was hit upon as a suitable material out of which the monetary unit can be fashioned by accident. Gold is heavy and shiny – an ideal symbol of opulence. Their failure to connect gold with senescence is all the more curious since Carl Menger, the founder of deductive economics had already developed the theory of marketability (*Absatzfähigkeit*) in the 19th century. He established the fact that gold had become money through a prolonged process of evolution making it far more marketable than any other good. This, apparently, failed to strike a sympathetic chord in von Mises. I am merely advocating a return to Menger and his 'quality theory of money'.

The disequilibrium theory of price

Von Mises was a professed quantity theorist. He readily admitted that the supply/demand equilibrium theory of price formation is a far cry from reality but, as he says, we have nothing better to replace it. As a penetrating study of Menger's work reveals, we actually do: the disequilibrium theory of price based on the bid/asked spread and its variation as a function of quantity.

Von Mises' addiction to the Quantity Theory of Money is all the more curious since he was an adamant opponent of positivism, a synonym for panphysicalism, a scheme designed to deny that there is any other method of scientific inquiry than empiricism. Historically, the Quantity Theory of Money is the most damaging fruit of panphysicalism.

Menger's 'Quality Theory of Money' is infinitely superior: the value of money, far from being determined by its quantity is, rather, determined by its *quality*, namely, the *quality of marketability*. [10]

Self-liquidating credit

The concept of self-liquidating credit has been around since the great scholars on banking theory introduced it in Germany in the 19th century. The source of self-liquidating credit is definitely not savings. Paradoxically, it is consumption, giving rise to discounting bills and to the discount rate. It should be thought of as the momentum that consumption, in particular consumption of goods most urgently demanded by the consumers, imparts to production. To von Mises demand is one dimensional. Although he agrees that Say's Law is valid: as long as people want to eat, there will be employment opportunities so that everyone who wants to earn wages, can. But he would not agree to the following extension of this proposition: as long as people want to eat, there will be an opportunity for everyone of character who has mastered the four rules of arithmetic to start his own retail business virtually without capital – thanks to the universal availability of self-liquidating credit. Street vendors can survive, indeed succeed, in front of the hypermarket. It's just a matter of moving goods from the producers to the consumers in the most efficient way (which hypermarkets may or may not be able to do). In more details: the movement of consumer goods being finished must be financed with the most marketable financial instrument second only to gold: the real bill.

From blockading trade to blocking bills

This fact is not merely of theoretical interest. For us, children of the 21st century, it is also a matter of preserving our civilisation. The disastrous experimentation with irredeemable currency has reached the point of no return. Our civilisation is at stake, and the only way to save it is through the gold coin standard cum real bills financing of trade. The bill market is the clearing house of the gold standard without which it cannot survive. This is why the British effort to go back on the gold standard in 1925 failed. After the peace treaty following World War I the victorious Entente powers could no longer blockade Germany's foreign trade. In their wisdom they instead blocked the circulation of international bills of exchange that used to finance it. In doing so they shot themselves in the foot as their own producers and consumers were equally handicapped by the forcible abolition of the multilateral trading system, that is, the international gold bill market. The victors in their blind hatred of German efficiency forced the straitjacket of the bilateral trading system on the whole world. This was tantamount to going back to barter – without realising it.

Destruction of the Wage Fund

In actual fact, it was even worse. The Entente Powers unwittingly destroyed the Wage Fund out of which workers (whose semi-finished products could not be sold for some 90 days while they 'mature' into finished products) had been paid. The forcible abolition of the international gold bill market made it impossible to continue paying wages to a great many workers. Economists were blind to see the dire consequences, the coming disaster in the form of the Great Depression of the 1930's and the unprecedented wave of unemployment in its wake. The only exception was Germany's professor *Heinrich Rittershausen,*[11] but his warnings were dismissed as German chauvinistic propaganda. The gold standard was made the whipping boy responsible for the catastrophic unemployment. That judgment is still outstanding. Just one economist, Wilhelm Röpke, had the courage to stand up and say that the fault lay not with the gold standard, but with those in whose care the gold standard was entrusted. The trouble was not with the gold standard per se, but with the decision to castrate it – by removing its clearing house, the gold bill market.

The ultimate extinguisher of debt

History is repeating itself. The present crisis is a gold crisis. Gold, the only ultimate extinguisher of debt has been unceremoniously deposed and exiled from the monetary system. In consequence debt in the world can only grow. Without gold there is no way to reduce the size of total debt. What they call debt reduction nowadays is just shifting debt from individuals to banks, from banks to governments, from governments, through their central banks, to the U.S. treasury where the buck stops. This is the most inane notion ever taking root among informed and intelligent people, raising questions how scores of Ivy League professors and Nobel prize laureates could treat it with respect. To camouflage the unlimited accumulation of unpaid and unpayable debt, excess debt is being kicked upstairs. It unobtrusively keeps accumulating as 'sovereign debt' of governments. Nevertheless, the holy name 'sovereign debt' does not neutralise its increasing toxicity.

The central bank is ordered to buy as much of the sovereign debt "as it takes" to contain deflation. However, money printing cannot keep up with the collapsing velocity of monetary circulation. The world is blindly rushing into another Great Depression and is facing another unprecedented wave of unemployment. The monetary authorities do see this coming. But whatever they do, their action is counterproductive. Deflation, which we may define as the spontaneous collapsing of the velocity of monetary circulation, continues and deepens – despite the printing spree. Central banks may print paper money to their hearts' content, but they are utterly helpless when it comes to controlling the velocity of circulation. They could not divine what people will do with the freshly printed paper money put into their hands (dropped from a helicopter). Central banks pray and hope that people will spend it on goods to prevent prices from falling. It is all in vain. Speculators front-run the central bank in buying the Treasury bonds. The appeal of risk-less profits is irresistible. They know the central bank is committed to a policy of open-ended bond purchases. Speculators pre-empt it in buying the bonds first.

Risk-free speculation

The hare-brained schemes of Keynes and Friedman assume that the only conceivable reaction of people to the stimulus of open-ended money-creation is: open-ended buying of goods – as falsely predicted by the Quantity Theory of Money. They failed to notice the fly in the ointment. The fly that has escaped their attention is risk-free speculation induced by the well-advertised open-market purchases of government debt by central banks. Open market purchases were hailed as a way to 'fine-tune' and 'micro-manage' the increase in the stock of money. We need not go into investigating the validity of the claim whether this is feasible or reasonable. It is sufficient to point out its fatal flaw: it ignores risk-free profits to which it inevitably gives rise. Rather than controlling the fall of prices, the policy of open market purchases contributes to the fall of interest rates through the exorbitant purchases of bonds by the speculators. However, falling interest rates, as this lecture series proves, erodes and ultimately destroys capital, thus deepening deflation and hatching depression.

The stealthy and illegal introduction of open market operations by the Federal Reserve in 1922 led to the ruination of the world economy. It did not take a century to accomplish this feat. It does more damage to civilisation than the NKVD and the Gestapo combined. It kills with invisible bullets.

In their obsession with the Quantity Theory of Money Keynes and Friedman forgot that the lure of risk-free profits would take precedence to the lure of consumption. People respond to the stimulus of open-ended money creation with open-ended purchases of Treasury paper – before they give thought to open-ended purchases of goods. The Fed sows inflation – only to reap deflation. On risk free bond speculation, see also Appendix.

After all is said and done, a durable regime of irredeemable currency, which Keynes and Friedman were so eager to establish, remains a pipe dream.

Munich, Bavaria, September 3, 2012.

Prof Antal E. Fekete

Acknowledgement

I want to express my thanks to the original sponsor of my book-writing project the fruit of which the kind reader now holds : Herr Johannes Müller of Bern, Switzerland, for his nigh infinite patience in waiting for the manuscript of this book and for his uncompromisingly high "perfectionist" standards.

My greatest debt is to my editor Peter Van Coppenolle, who is my student of longest standing, for writing the handsome foreword and for taking care of all the printing arrangements.

In the last touches of this manuscript my student David van der Linden provided great help.

Budapest, Hungary, August 28, 2016

Prof. Antal E. Fekete

About the author

Antal E. Fekete, Professor, Memorial University of Newfoundland, was born in Budapest, Hungary, in 1932. He graduated from the Loránt Eötvös University of Budapest in mathematics in 1955. He left Hungary in the wake of the 1956 anti-Communist uprising that was brutally put down by the occupying Soviet troops. He immigrated to Canada in the following year and was appointed Assistant Professor at the Memorial University of Newfoundland in 1958. In 1993, after 35 years' of service he retired with the rank of Full Professor. During this period he also had tours of duty as visiting professor at Columbia University in the City of New York (1961), Trinity College, Dublin, Ireland (1964), Acadia University, Wolfville, Nova Scotia (1970), Princeton University, Princeton, New Jersey (1974). Since 2005 he has been Professor at Large of Intermountain Institute for Science and Applied Mathematics (IISAM), Missoula, Montana.

Professor Fekete is an autodidactic expert on monetary economics. During his associations with various universities and institutions he has done research and lectured on economics. On one such occasion, in 1974, he gave a talk on gold in the seminar of Paul Volcker, then Senior Fellow at Princeton University, soon to be named as President of the Federal Reserve Bank of New York and, later, as Chairman of the Federal Reserve Board.

In 1984 Professor Fekete was invited by the American Institute for Economic Research in Great Barrington, Massachusetts, to spend a year there as Visiting Fellow. He served as Editor of the Monograph Series of the Committee for Monetary Research and Education, then headquartered in Greenwich, Connecticut, while contributing several monographs to the Series, reproduced on this website. He also acted as Senior Editor for the American Economic Foundation in Cleveland, Ohio, and produced the popular pamphlet series Ten Pillars of Sound Money, also reproduced on this website. When in 1984 South Africa celebrated the 100th anniversary of discovering gold in the Witwatersrand, at the conference Gold 100 commemorating that event in Johannesburg Professor Fekete delivered the keynote address entitled Gold in the International Monetary System, also reproduced on this website.

In 1985 Congressman William E. Dannemeyer of Fullerton, California, invited Professor Fekete to join his staff in Washington, D.C., to work on fiscal and monetary reform. While on this assignment, lasting for five years, he gave numerous lectures on Capitol Hill as well as in California. Ultimately the proposals hammered out in Congressional offices under his chairmanship were taken to the White House by a delegation of ten Republican Congressmen led by Congressman Dannemeyer. According to these proposals the runaway government deficit could be reined in by refinancing the entire U.S. government debt through issuing gold bonds. The historic meeting took place in the Oval Office in October, 1989, and was duly reported by The New York Times. Having listened attentively to the presentation of Mr. Dannemeyer, President George Bush, Sr., instructed his Treasury Secretary, also present at the meeting, to let the Congressional and Treasury staff meet and put forward a joint proposal. This initiative came to nought as the Treasury deliberately derailed negotiations through procrastination.

About the editor

Peter Van Coppenolle graduated in law and economics from Johannesburg University in 1986 and from Brussels, Tilburg & Leuven Universities (LLM International Tax) in 2009 & 2010. After graduating, he worked as a researcher for the South African Foreign Trade Organisation and for Barlows in the finance department. In Brussels, Peter served for a number of Belgian public and private companies either as director or advisor. He is currently a partner of Pintax cvba, an independent tax and legal advisory service, specialising in succession planning for the disabled. Peter has been a student of Austrian Economics since 1990 and an assistant lecturer of Prof. Antal Fekete since 2001. His expertise is predominantly in the establishment of solid protection devices for succession planning, especially suited for needy or disabled loved ones.

Peter is a lecturer and researcher at the the New Austrian School of Economics (NASoE). He is also fellow and honorary board member of Fekete Research Ltd. in London. His predilection is for Greek philosophy and philosophy of mind.

Professor Fekete was himself senior chief editor for the American Economic Foundation. And for good reason. His texts hardly need editing. Intervention was limited to providing endnotes, some graphs, a bit of text styling and compiling an index.

Contents

List of Abbreviations

CIA : Central Intelligence Agency
F.R. : Federal Reserve
GDP : Gross Domestic Product
Gestapo: Geheime Staatspolizei (Nazi Germany Secret Service)
GM ™ : General Motors ™
IBM ™ : International Business Machines ™
IMF : International Monetary Fund
NASoE : New Austrian School of Economics
NKVD: Narodnij Komissariat Vnoetrennich Djel (USSR Secret Service)
QTM : Quantity Theory of Money
SCC : Social Circulating Capital
US : United States (of America)
UK : United Kingdom

Table of Figures

Chapter 1. Marginal Utility and Unit Price

I introduce my subject with a simple example that has been overlooked. The word 'price' is being used in a sloppy and imprecise way. Actually, it should always mean 'unit price', yet often it is used to mean 'total price' of a consignment. Carl Menger (1840 – 1921), the father of the Austrian School of Economics set out to clear up the confusion. Quantity theorists assume that total price increases linearly as a function of quantity. Twice, three times, four etc. times as much costs twice, three times, four etc. times as much [See Figure 1A infra p. 4]. Of course, this means that the unit price is constant [See Figure 1B infra p. 4]. Menger realised that this was a crude distortion of facts. It never happens (save one important instance as we shall soon see). In general, total price is an increasing non-linear function of quantity. It gets larger but by ever smaller amounts [See Figure 2A infra, p. 5]. Nonlinearity is a fact of life. When you buy one egg, they make you pay a higher unit price than what you pay when you buy eggs by the dozen. The unit price is not constant: it is decreasing with quantity [See Figure 2B infra p. 5]. In a market where supply is not discrete as in the egg market, but continuous as in the flour market, we recognise that the unit price is just the differential quotient of the price: it is the rate of change in the variation of the total price.

I criticise mainstream Austrian economics for paying lip service to the Principle of Marginal Utility without embracing its substance. To see this I review the historical background. Menger wanted to axiomatise the common experience that the increase of total price is nonlinear, and the unit price is a declining function of quantity. He ran into a vicious loop. To measure values he needed a measuring rod. He could not have one without finding the material first out of which he could fabricate it. However, he could find it only if he were able to measure value already. To escape from the vicious loop Menger introduced the ideas of utility and marginal utility. Utility connotes with total price; marginal utility, with unit price.

At this point Menger introduced two key postulates:

- Postulate of increasing utility.

  The economising individual, when confronted with the choice between two different supplies of the same economic good, will choose the larger.

- Postulate of declining marginal utility.

  The economising individual, in acquiring subsequent units of a supply of the same economic good, will earmark units acquired later with a lower priority, while those acquired earlier are earmarked with a higher priority.

If the supply is continuous rather than discrete, then we recognise that marginal utility is just the differential quotient of utility, that is, the rate of change in the variation of utility. This enables us to rank all goods according to the rate of decline of marginal utility (assigning higher rank to the lower rate of decline). Then the good having the highest rank (lowest rate of decline) will play a most important role in the evolution of the market economy. Over long periods of time it will be promoted to the status of money. This good behaves exactly like all goods are supposed to behave in the warped view of quantity theorists, [see Figures 1A and 1B *infra* p. 4]. In other words, the marginal utility of money declines so slowly that for all practical purposes it can be taken to be (nonzero) constant. Consequently the utility of money is proportional to its quantity. Moreover, money is the only good that behaves this way.

In markets where the supply of goods changes continuously (as opposed to changing discretely), utility and marginal utility behave much like total price and unit price do: the increase in utility is nonlinear, while marginal utility declines with increasing quantity [see Figures 2A and 2B *infra* p. 5].

The particular good that has over the millennia evolved to become money, love it or hate it – is gold. It is thanks to gold that we can measure value, have prices, and we can do economic calculation. This was the greatest breakthrough in the history of economics.

It became the new foundation of the theory of value where all the greatest minds, including Adam Smith, went astray. Since antiquity everybody has assumed that value could be measured by the amount of work needed to produce it.[12] Karl Marx borrowed Adam Smith's idea and came up with a theory of exploitation. The toiling masses are ruthlessly exploited by the owners of capital, who unjustly expropriate the 'surplus value' labour has produced. In Lenin's hand the word became flesh,[13] and millions of innocent people (some shot, others starved to death) were "liquidated" before the mistake could be corrected.

Nowadays doctrinaire Keynesians and Friedmanites, in denying that gold is a nature-given[14] measure of value, deny marginal utility. They promote the dogma of government omnipotence in matters of choosing the monetary unit, defying the market's choice.[15]

Not surprisingly, the government always chooses its own debt as the basis for the monetary system.

How many hundreds of millions of more innocent people will have to die inside or outside of the Gulag in the last-ditch defence of this vicious dogma?

More on marginal utility can be found in Chapter 7

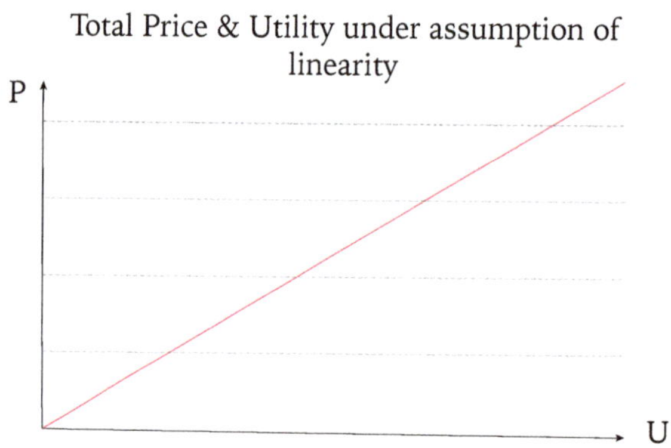

Figure 1 A

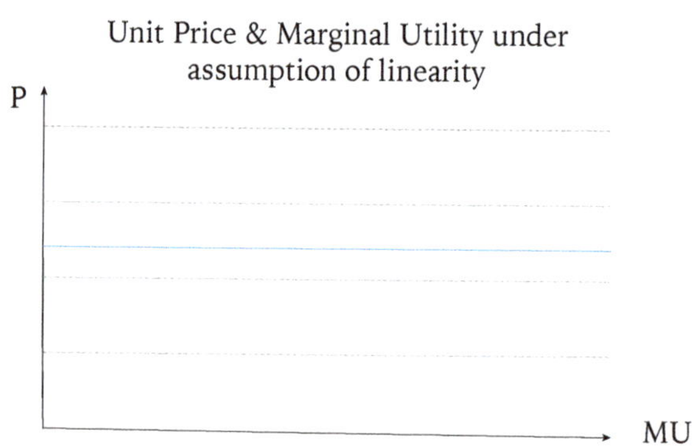

Figure 1 B

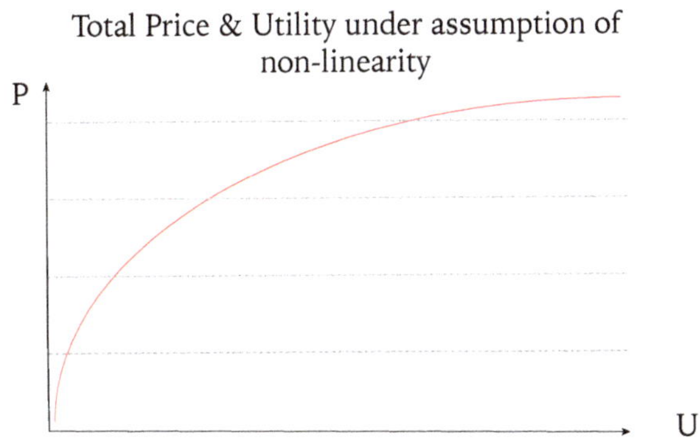

Figure 2 A

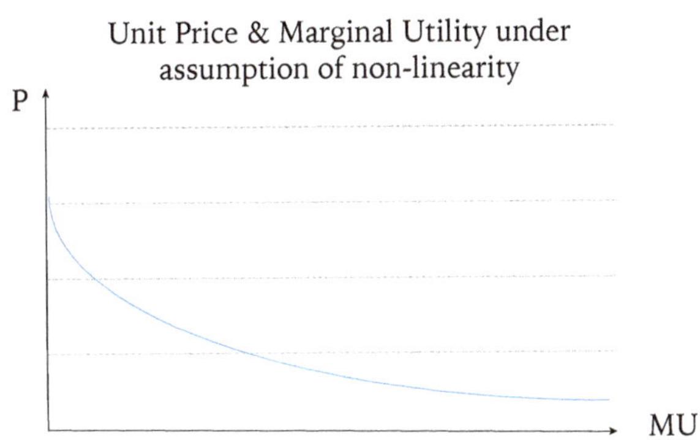

Figure 2 B

Chapter 2. Marginal Productivity of Labour

It is curious that von Mises does not deal systematically with the marginal productivity of labour and with the marginal productivity of capital in his major treatises. Besides reading it, I have run a search engine on Human Action and found only asides. These fundamental concepts do crop up in a minor essay of his: The Anti-capitalistic Mentality, first published in 1956. Marginal productivity of capital is barely mentioned; marginal productivity of labour is treated hurriedly. According to von Mises the concept of productivity of labour is nonsensical. It refers to an undefined and undefinable quantity. We have to talk about the marginal productivity of labour, he says, i.e., *"the deduction in net output to be caused by the elimination of one worker. Then it refers to a definite economic quantity, or its equivalent in money."* [16]

This, however, still does not remove ambiguity. The elimination of which worker? Why, the marginal worker, naturally. But von Mises does not say who the marginal worker is. To clarify the matter we change the negative definition of von Mises to its positive equivalent. Marginal productivity of labour is defined as the addition to net output to be caused by the hiring of the marginal worker, i.e., the worker whose contribution, while lower than that of those already hired, is higher than that of others seeking employment (submarginal workers).

This definition is still unsatisfactory. The marginal worker is not a person; it is a role to be cast. The cast is subject to change without notice. We rank all workers according to their productivity, that is, according to the increase in output that hiring each would contribute to the success of the enterprise. To be sure, workers do have their individual productivity. The marginal worker's productivity is just high enough so that it will make a positive contribution to the success of the enterprise. He will be the first to be employed. The rest whose productivity is lower will not be: their hiring would cause losses to the enterprise. The productivity of the marginal worker is called the marginal productivity of labour. The concept of marginal worker is meaningful even if no hiring or firing takes place.

This concept is important because *it alone determines the wage rate.* Wages are not fixed by the employer capriciously. They are determined by the consumers who may buy or refuse to buy the consumer good. If a worker's productivity is submarginal, it means that the consumers will not compensate the employer for the outlay of his wages, causing a loss. No enterprise can go on making losses while hoping to stay in business. Public opinion calling this selection cruel or inhuman notwithstanding, the fact remains that the right to work is not a birthright. The 'blame' belongs to the consumer who refuses to pay top dollar for low quality or mispriced merchandise. This consumer behaviour is universal: the submarginal worker himself behaves accordingly when he goes shopping.

Note the common features of the definitions of marginal utility and marginal productivity of labour. Most conspicuous is what we call the Method of Marginalism replacing the Method of Averaging. In both cases there is a ranking: subjects are ranked according to given criteria. The marginal subject emerges as the last person who just meets the criterion.

The great insight of Menger was that economics is dealing with the contact points between the logosphere [17] (the sphere of reason) and the protosphere (defined by combining the geosphere and the subhuman biosphere). In the latter the Method of Averaging is appropriate and paramount. In the former it is useless: we must have recourse to the Method of Marginalism.

The concept of marginal productivity of labour demonstrates the futility of government policy of high wages. The government may introduce minimum wage legislation (ostensibly to protect employees against the greed of employers). It may legalise violence: grant unions power to force fellow workers reluctant to join strike action. It may also allow the use of violence against company property.

Government policy and union violence may indeed prevent employers from hiring workers at a wage determined by the labour market.

But it cannot force employers to hire at uneconomic wages. All that government policy and union violence will accomplish is to raise the marginal productivity of labour artificially and unnecessarily, thereby pushing ever more people into the submarginal category. Government policy and union violence are among the chief causes of unemployment today.

Chapter 3. Marginal Productivity of Capital

The absence of a systematic treatment of the marginal productivity of capital in Human Action is even more conspicuous. "Marginal productivity of the material factors of production" is mentioned in *The Anti-Capitalist Mentality* by L. von Mises, (1972 edition, p. 86), but that is all.

Let us define the marginal productivity of capital as the increase in net output to be caused by the application of the marginal capital good. In more detail, we rank all material factors of production according to their productivity. The productivity of X is the increase in net output caused by the application of X per total dollar cost of installing it. In other words, the marginal productivity of the material factor of production X is the quota of increase in net output that can be attributed to $1 of the total cost of installing it.

The marginal capital good is that material factor of production the contribution of which, while lower than those applied already, is higher than any alternative not in use. It is the first material factor of production that will be applied as soon as production is expanded. The rest whose productivity is lower will not be: their employment would cause losses to the enterprise. These factors are called submarginal. The productivity of the marginal capital good is called the marginal productivity of capital. Again, we should think about marginal capital not as a definite plant or piece of equipment but, rather, as a role to be cast. The cast is subject to change without notice. Even if no change in the park of capital goods is contemplated, marginal capital has a role to play.

The concept of the marginal productivity of capital is important because of its role in the formation of the rate of interest. This is the subject of chapter 16. The marginal entrepreneur is doing arbitrage between the bond market and the market for capital goods. If the rate of interest rises above the rate of marginal productivity of capital, then he is the first to sell his capital goods and use the proceeds (and savings from suspended capital maintenance) to buy the bond.

Bonds are cheap, their yield is higher than the return he could earn from production. Conversely, if the rate of interest retreats sufficiently, then the marginal entrepreneur will sell bonds from portfolio at a profit, buy back (and restart the maintenance of) his capital goods, and reboot production. We shall say that the marginal productivity of capital determines the ceiling for the range in which the rate of interest may move. (The floor is determined by marginal time preference, i.e., the time preference of the marginal bondholder doing arbitrage between the bond market and the gold market. [See charts on p. 68]. This is the subject of Chapter 17.)

This interplay between the change of the interest rate and contraction - expansion in production is well known and has been discussed by several authors (possibly using different terminology), among others by von Hayek in his book *Prices and Production*. It is all the more surprising that von Mises categorically refuses to admit that marginal productivity of capital has anything at all to do with the variation in rate of interest. In fact he chastised Eugene Böhm-Bawerk for including a chapter in his great work *Capital and Interest* surveying the productivity theories of interest (having surveyed the time preference theories of interest in an earlier chapter). Böhm-Bawerk was right to keep productivity theories in the fold. There is no real antagonism here. Instead, we have the possibility for synthesis between the two rival theories, as motivated by Carl Menger's seminal idea of the bid/asked spread. We shall return to this in Chapter 18.

NASoE has been the first to spell out this synthesis in a single unified theory of interest. In the light of this, 'management' of the rate of interest by the central bank is seen to cause capital erosion, in the extreme case, capital destruction. The process is most insidious. It is camouflaged as a 'benevolent interference' nudging the economy towards full employment by making the rate of interest lower. In fact, however, a prolonged fall in the interest-rate structure is lethal. It inevitably induces falling prices. It imperceptibly destroys capital, causing wholesale bankruptcies and unemployment. It leads to depression.

Every entrepreneur in trying to make a positive investment decision is doomed under a falling interest-rate structure. He has made his decision at the wrong time. Another entrepreneur who was smart enough to wait for the rate of interest to fall more will have the edge: his cost of capital is going to be lower. The trouble is that a third one who waited even longer will be able to borrow at an even lower rate. He will beat them both.[18] The conclusion is that, under a permanently falling interest rate structure no rational decision to make an investment can be made. All investments are doomed: all capital is being eroded just as soon as installed. Moreover, it is eroded at a rate faster than the natural erosion due to wear and tear. The ultimate result is total capital destruction.

The present official 'zero interest rate policy' (ZIRP) of the Fed endangers the very survival of our civilisation. It is an insane policy, inspired and guided by an insane theory, Keynesianism with its characteristic denigration of capital.[19] In the 20th century capital destruction was manifested by 'outsourcing', as was called the wholesale export of jobs from America and Europe to China and elsewhere.

Capital goods are not the only ones subject to erosion[20] as described above. Financial capital is equally at stake as shown by the Great Financial Crisis that started in 2007-2008. It will continue relentlessly as long as the policy of serial halving of interest rates continues.

It is questionable that this policy can be stopped and reversed: we have reached and passed the point of no return. The talk about "exit strategy" and "tapering" is mere whistling in the dark. The mirror image of interest rates falling to zero is bond prices going to infinity, as manifested by the quadrillion-dollar [21] strong derivatives tower that feeds upon itself. The game of musical chairs must go on, but a game of musical chairs it shall remain.

We shall return to the problem of capital destruction caused by the falling interest rate structure in Chapter 20.

After having introduced the ideas of marginal productivity of labour and capital separately, they can be brought together. Firstly it should be noted that the ideas of labour and capital cannot be contemplated separately from each other. This becomes apparent in realising that a capital item forms the workers' tools. These tools can only be considered productive in the hands of the worker.

So it can be seen that new capital and labour must be employed together. The marginal role is played both at the retirement of a worker and his tools, and at the employment of newly trained labour and newly developed tools.

We may recall that in discussing the marginal productivity of labour, we replaced von Mises' negative definition with a positive one. We do not consider the deduction in output caused by the elimination of the marginal worker, but rather the addition to output to be caused by the introduction of the marginal worker.

In the above, these definitions have been merged, since the marginal worker and his tools are replaced at retirement with newly trained workers and their tools entering the workforce. We can now talk about (1) the marginal worker (*apprentice*) and (2) the marginal worker (*retiree*). Likewise we may talk about (1) the marginal capital good (to be phased-in) and (2) the marginal capital good (to be phased-out). This refinement of the adjective "marginal" puts into high relief *the dynamics of the change in the labour force and in the stock of capital goods*.

Chapter 4. Marginal Time Preference

The corner stone of von Mises' theory of interest is his concept of originary interest.[22] Human beings value any good available immediately more highly than an identical good available only in the future. For von Mises, this is an apodictic rule that brooks no exception. He is using the example of an apple. If available only a year hence, it may be worth, say, just three quarters of an apple available immediately. The discounted value of the apple one year hence is obtained by multiplying the present value by the discount factor which, in this case, is $3/4$. A simple calculation, not reproduced here, shows that the discounted value of the apple 2, 3, … , n years hence is = $(3/4)^2$, $(3/4)^3$,…, $(3/4)^n$. This is a decreasing sequence since the discount factor is less than 1. In general, if the discount factor is $q < 1$, the discounted future value in n years, due to time preference, is q^n. We say that future value is subject to the Law of Exponential Decay (according to von Mises' concept of time discount).

Von Mises' proposition on time discount is questionable. Even if we stay within the realm of the apple orchard, we encounter exceptions. Consider an isolated apple orchard that has been destroyed by a landslide just after apple harvest. There is no other apple orchard in the vicinity. In this case an apple available a year hence will be valued more highly, not less, than an identical apple immediately available.

This is not a freak example like that of ice-in-summer / ice-in-winter. We have a whole range of them. Consider that a new observatory is to be built on an isolated mountain top. The target date for opening is a year from now. There are two major components involved in the project:

(1) the building to house the telescope;
(2) the telescope itself.

Through delays in the construction of the building the target date has to be postponed by one year, while the delivery of the telescope is made on time.

Questions:

> What is the present value of the telescope at the time of delivery to the site?
>
> How does it compare with the value of the same telescope on the new target date a year later, that is, when the building is completed and ready to receive it?

Clearly, there is no future discount here. The telescope must be stored and insured for an additional year at extra cost that must come out of its present value. As a result, the present value will be at a discount; the future value will be at a premium.

We have seen that von Mises' assumption of an automatic future discount on all goods is equivalent to the statement that future value is subject to the Law of Exponential Decay. While declining, the future discounted value is always positive. But as our telescope example shows, in general it may not be. Moreover, the future discounted value may or may not vary along an exponential curve. Generally it is a U-shaped curve with the bottom corresponding to a negative value in case of a delay in completing the building (or in case of early delivery of the telescope). Similar examples can be constructed for products with two or more major components. If the delivery of these components is not dovetailed exactly, then extra costs such as storage and insurance may distort the schedule of future values.

We may conclude that the assumption of an apodictic discount on future values cannot be a valid basis for the theory of interest. Originary interest is a phantom. The future is a closed book to us. We just don't know how people, ourselves included, will value goods in the future. Our value system may change as time goes on.

Upon closer scrutiny we find that there is but one type of assets for which von Mises' assumption on automatic future discount is unconditionally applicable, namely, debt. The future value of a non-performing loan follows the Law of Exponential Decay. This forces us to consider debt markets (typically the bond market where evidences of debt are traded) for clues as to the variation of the rate of interest.

After all has been said and done, the formation of the rate of interest turns out to be a market process, contrary to what von Mises had to say on the subject. The rate of interest by its nature is a price, and it is formed in the markets in the same manner as prices of goods are formed. We must abandon all previous definitions and redefine the rate of interest in terms of the bond price as follows:

> *The rate of interest at any given time is that rate at which the stream of coupon payments (representing periodic payments of interest without amortisation) plus the repayment of the principal sum at maturity amortise the market value (as distinct from the face value) of the bond.*

We are now ready to develop a new theory of interest in the spirit of Menger, which makes the rate of interest the outcome of a market process. (See also: Chapters 16 and 19.)

Let us now show that the Axiom of Time Preference, properly interpreted, is equivalent to von Mises' statement that the rate of interest, properly defined, is always positive. Man has to save in order to survive. He cannot consume now and save later, unless someone else is doing the saving first, voluntarily (as in the case of one's parents) or involuntarily (as in the case of one's slaves). Interest immediately arises in connection with saving. The primitive method of saving is through hoarding. Hoardability is an indispensable property of commodities to consider when converting *income into wealth and wealth into income*. The efficiency of hoarding cannot be further improved once the most hoardable substance, gold (or silver) is employed.

But the efficiency of conversion can still be improved further if we pass from direct conversion to indirect conversion of income and wealth; that is, from hoarding to exchange. Direct conversion means gold hoarding and dishoarding. It can be effected by the saver all by himself. It has the disadvantage that the amounts involved are severely limited. These limits are removed once we pass from the direct to the indirect method of conversion. That is, if instead of hoarding we use exchange. The disadvantage is that in this case conversion takes two: one who gives up wealth (the provider of credit), and the other who gives up income (the user of credit). It is here that interest puts in its first appearance. Zero interest means that the gold of the provider of credit exchanges exactly the same weight and fineness of gold that the user of credit is paying back piecemeal. In reality such an exchange never takes place because the provider of credit has no incentive to make it. As already pointed out, he is free to make the conversion all by himself (through hoarding and dishoarding, without the hassle of carting, and facing the risk of losing some gold in the process). Positive interest is needed to furnish the necessary incentive for the provider of credit to go ahead with the exchange. Parties to the exchange do not have the same bargaining power. That of the user of credit is impaired in comparison with that of the provider of credit. Those who find it inequitable, can blame it on mother nature. That's the way the world is ordained, like it or not. We may formulate this as an axiom:

> THE AXIOM OF TIME PREFERENCE. *If an economising individual is offered the choice of two consignments of gold of the same weight and fineness, the first is payable as a lump sum here and now; the second is payable piecemeal over a period of time in the future, then he will choose the first.*

It is not hard to see that this axiom is equivalent to that of von Mises stipulating that zero rate of interest is not possible.

Chapter 5. Marginal Productivity of Debt

In Chapter 2 we introduced the concepts of protosphere (the geosphere plus subhuman biosphere) and the logosphere where reason and human action are also present (the point where we leave the world of causality and enter the world of teleology.)[23] We have also seen several examples how to use Menger's Method of Marginalism (as distinct from the mathematical Method of Averaging) to introduce important new concepts such as, for example, the marginal productivity of capital. Generally speaking, the Method of Averaging is applicable in the protosphere, but may fail in the logosphere. This important limitation on the applicability of mathematical methods was not recognised before Carl Menger. The merit is his: Menger was the first to realise that, thanks to the power of reasoning, human beings can change the database even while doing the calculation. Of course, this will falsify the bottom line. Averages and teleology do not mix. There is need for a new method to supplement the old: the Method of Marginalism. Von Mises, while recognising the all-important difference between causality and teleology, failed to realise that subjectivism goes way beyond marginal utility and the theory of value. There is a whole range of contact points between the protosphere and the logosphere where the Method of Marginalism supersedes the Method of Averaging. As we have seen, von Mises barely touches upon these points of contact. He failed to work out the concept of the marginal productivity of labour and capital in sufficient detail. [24]

Above all, von Mises failed to work out the concept of marginal time preference. He talked about time preference as if it were the average time preference of individuals (somewhere between the time preference of Scrooge and that of the prodigal son). However, as Menger showed, the Method of Averages might be inapplicable in the logosphere. Von Mises should have used the Method of Marginalism. Here is how he should have proceeded. Having ranked all bondholders according to their time preference, he should have focused on the marginal bondholder who is the first to trade his future good (the gold bond) for a present good (the gold coin) as the rate of interest drops further. He will keep the proceeds in the form of gold coins in protest against the low-interest policy of the banks.

The Method of Marginalism is applied by von Mises in the case of the marginal productivity of labour. The ranking involved is that according to productivity. The marginal productivity of labour is just the productivity of the marginal worker. He is the one who gets hired first in case the production effort is expanded. Observe the contact point between the protosphere and the logosphere: *the marginal subject*. We have seen in Chapter 2 that the marginal subject is not a person: it is a role to be cast. In case of fast technological changes the cast will change frequently. The same procedure can be used for defining the marginal productivity of capital as the productivity of the marginal factor of production, see Chapter 3. Here the contact point between the protosphere and the logosphere is *the marginal object*. Again, it is not a physical object, but a role to be cast. At the time of fast technological changes the cast can change often.

The Method of Marginalism has not been extended to cover all economics. That is a pity: we could conceptualise the whole spectrum of human action using the same methodology. In Chapter 20 we shall discuss the concept of the marginal productivity of social circulating capital extending the Method of Marginalism to Adam Smith's Real Bills Doctrine. Thus we develop the theory of discount in a novel way. Such an approach is badly needed since, following von Mises, a large number of economists today denies the existence of a discount rate as distinct from that of the rate of interest.

We proceed to discuss the concept of marginal productivity of debt. Nowadays it is fashionable to argue that there is nothing alarming about the quantity of debt outstanding, because what matters is the GDP/debt ratio. After all, the larger the GDP, the greater amount of debt the economy may carry. By historical standards, present GDP per debt levels in the U.S. and the U.K. are not extreme, and the monetary authorities are more than able to handle them. They will reduce debt levels once they kick-start the economy through further reducing the rate of interest.

Whatever the GDP/debt ratio measures, it cannot measure the debt-carrying ability of the economy. The proper ratio to watch is the marginal productivity of debt, or ΔGDP/Δdebt (additional wealth created by $1 dollar worth of additional debt). The question is how much additional wealth is produced at the margin. In the decade following World War II the marginal productivity of debt was greater than 2. As long as it is greater than 1, the economy is working fine. Every dollar of new debt creates more than one dollar's worth of new wealth on a net basis. Trouble starts when the marginal productivity of debt starts falling towards 1. At 1 no new wealth is being created net of debt.

For the sake of argument we ignore the fact that the GDP may include a lot of hot air. For example, it is suggested that doubling the size of the civil service would add greatly to wealth – a dubious proposition. Be that as it may, when the marginal productivity of debt is less than 1 but still positive, going deeper into debt has lost all its conceivable economic justification. It no longer pays for itself in terms of new wealth creation.

But the red alert signal comes when the marginal productivity of debt goes negative. It means that going deeper into debt is destroying existing wealth. The economy is sucked into the black hole. All measures the monetary authorities may take will from then on be counter- productive. The debt-creating machine is spinning out of control.

Two analysts studying the marginal productivity of debt agree that it has been falling consistently since 1971, the year when the U.S. defaulted on its international gold obligations. The fall has been accelerating and the marginal productivity of debt is approaching zero. One analyst puts the date of this ominous event at 2015; according to the other it has already happened at the start of the Great Financial Crisis in 2007/2008. [25] Whatever the correct date is, we are now in a very dangerous situation. Most alarming is the fact that policymakers, while they may have the correct diagnosis of deflation, apply the wrong medicine, the monetisation of government debt, that makes deflation worse, not better, regardless whether or not hyperinflation is in the cards.

(For the purposes of this analysis we may define hyperdeflation as the pathological dystrophy of the velocity of money. The opposite malady is hyperinflation, the pathological hypertrophy of the velocity of money.)

Let us summarise the events of the past 40 years. After the U.S. defaulted on its gold obligations in 1971, gold was thoughtlessly removed from the international monetary system. In this way the only ultimate extinguisher of debt was discarded. Ever since debt is created without any regard to its economic usefulness (or to its economic toxicity). Total debt can only increase, never contract. At one point the marginal productivity of debt will turn negative, if it hasn't already. Thereafter additional debt is pure poison. Wealth and capital are being destroyed at an accelerating rate. Poverty spreads. Law and order will break down. As an act of criminal negligence, the economic profession failed to examine the ultimate consequences of the world-wide experiment with fiat money, in spite of the fact that such experiments in the past had a 100% failure rate. This unprecedented experiment that will wreak havoc on the world economy.

Chapter 6. From Price to Spread. Human Action is Arbitrage

Traditionally economics is about price; it is about buying and selling. Von Mises gave the title Human Action to his magnum opus and he described the purposive action of humans to remove felt uneasiness through producing goods and services, and trading them in the markets. There is nothing wrong with this description. However, the overview of economics can be greatly simplified and at the same time made more penetrating if, instead of focusing on the price (which is pretty meaningless in and of itself) we focus on the spread (which is more encompassing). Then the meaning of human action is also simplified. It is arbitrage: buying in one market and selling in another. The spread is the sale price minus the purchase price. Note that in general the spread (unlike its special case, the bid/asked spread) can be negative. Buying and selling need not be simultaneous, nor has buying to precede selling (i.e., short selling is permissible). Buying and selling may be done in the same or in different markets. To streamline terminology we shall use the language of long and short legs of a straddle. Typically, a long leg is a purchase, but it can also be the covering (offsetting) of a short position. Correspondingly, a short leg is a sale, but it can also be the offsetting of a long position. In this view economic activity appears as shuffling of straddles.[26]

A *straddle* is a combination of a number of long and short legs (the numbers may or may not be equal). The spread belonging to the straddle is defined as follows. Each straddle has an opposite straddle obtained by reversing every leg (a long leg is replaced by the equivalent short leg, and a short leg by the equivalent long). Thus the opposite straddle offsets the original: the position of the market actor becomes neutral when he offsets his straddles. Because the selling price of the earlier purchase, or the covering price of the earlier short sale could be different from the prices at which these positions have been initiated, offsetting may cause the ledger to change. The spread of the straddle is the value of short legs minus the value of the long. Profit or loss occurs according as the spread of the straddle is positive or negative. The name of the game is to make 'straddle-farming' as profitable as possible.

The concept of a straddle is to be taken in its most general sense. Thus we can talk about one-legged straddles. For example, take the case of an entrepreneur replacing one of the inputs A of his production effort with another B by shifting custom. This transaction is regarded as a one-legged straddle with long leg B (while the short leg A that cancels the standing order for A is considered a 'phantom long leg'). In another example, a housewife starts buying a new household item X that has just come on the market. Hers is also a one-legged straddle with long leg X. Again, there is a 'phantom short leg' Y which is the nearest substitute for X. In this way the production and distribution of goods appears as a landscape of straddles and spreads that, properly cultivated, will generate profits for the market participants.

Arbitrage in its most primitive form appears as barter 'telescoping' as it were the long and short legs into a single transaction. Further examples: the market-maker is doing arbitrage between the bid and asked price causing the bid/asked spread to contract. Import/export business is arbitrage between the domestic and the overseas markets. This shows that one can do arbitrage between two different markets separated in space. Markets for future delivery show that one can do arbitrage between markets separated in time. The most complex business transactions can be described in terms of arbitrage: the entrepreneur sets up a straddle with several long and short legs; then he works on his straddle through a series of arbitrage operations aiming to offset it later.

Curiously, von Mises has no use for the word 'arbitrage'. Checking the index of Human Action reveals just one entry, and it refers to an aside.[27] Von Mises keeps talking about buying and selling at market prices to make a profit, rather than talking about setting up straddles and doing arbitrage with the aim to offset them later at positive spreads.

NASoE is championing a paradigm-shift from prices to spreads and from buying or selling to arbitrage. The possibility of changing the spread through arbitrage to a more profitable one is what animates human action. Thus we have a more comprehensive view of the market process. It also allows a glimpse into the mind of the entrepreneur. His secret is to find the most promising straddles which he can husband, through a series of arbitrage operations, before offsetting them at the greatest positive spread (profit). The conventional supply/demand equilibrium model of economics is obsolete. It ought to be replaced by the more up-to-date model of the landscape of all straddles and spreads, which is the stage on which the drama of human action is played out.

In fact, if we return to Menger's theory of exchange, we find that arbitrage forms its basis. This is made clear in understanding the idea of declining marginal utility. Menger's own example is about two neighbouring farms, a granary and a vineyard, each with a surplus of their respective produce. The grain farmer realises that he can take his last bushel to his neighbour and exchange it for the latter's last cask. In doing so, the last bushel has become the first available at the neighbour's farm. Likewise, at the granary, the last cask has become the first. Thus it becomes clear that declining marginal utility forms the basis for a spread to be arbitraged.

Chapter 7. Menger's Concept of Marketability

In current textbooks on Austrian economics Menger's concept of marketability appears fuzzy, even ambiguous. For example, some authors define marketability in terms of the cost (both in time and money) of "liquidating" (read: selling) the item under consideration that has been purchased earlier. Ambiguity can be avoided if we reduce the concept of marketability to the most pivotal idea of Menger: the spread. "Marketability" is used here as shorthand for "marketability in the large" or "saleability" (*Absatzfähigkeit*) that is at the heart of the theory of value. ("Marketability in the small" or "hoardability" is at the heart of the theory of interest, and is dealt with in Chapter 18.) In what follows, the word 'item' shall mean either a good or a paper asset actively traded in the markets. Both concepts, marketability in the large and marketability in the small refer to the rate of change of the bid/asked spread as a function of quantity. The bid/asked spread of an item A is asked price minus bid price. Since the asked price is always higher than the bid price , the bid/asked spread is always positive. We say that the item A is more marketable than another B if the bid/asked spread of A is increasing more slowly than that of B as ever larger quantities of A and B are thrown on the market. For example, the share of the firm IBM is more marketable than the share of GM (because GM has been through a bankruptcy procedure; IBM has not). Another example is tobacco that is more marketable than hay (because saturation of the hay market occurs more frequently).

There are problems with this definition. It appears to be circular. A spread assumes prices, and prices assume the measurability of value in terms of the most marketable good, the concept we are trying to define. Menger introduced the concept of marginal utility precisely in order to eliminate this circularity. As we have seen in Chapter 1 the concept of marginal utility involves an object (a certain good or asset X) and a subject (the market actor). The latter strives to acquire (through production or through barter) more units of the former, but will do so ever more reluctantly as his inventory of X is getting larger, until he reaches his satiation point beyond which he does not want to acquire any more units of X. In more technical language we say that the utility of his inventory increases with quantity (up to his satiation point, where it becomes stationary). The marginal utility of X is defined as the utility of an additional unit of X to the marginal actor (i.e., the actor who has not reached his satiation point, but will do so upon the acquisition of just one more unit of X, when the marginal utility of X to him becomes zero).

All items (goods or assets) have declining marginal utilities. They can be ranked according to the rate of decline. The highest rank belongs to the item whose marginal utility declines at the slowest rate. Unit quantity of this particular item will serve as the unit of value. The value of all other items can be expressed as a multiple or a fraction of this unit. Equipped with a suitable unit of value we have unit prices for A and B, we have bid/asked spreads, and we can measure and compare the variation of spreads. As it happens, gold is the first (and silver the second) most marketable good. Saying it differently, the satiation point for gold is farther away than that for any other marketable item. So far away indeed that for all practical purposes it is beyond reach. (The process just described is like that of selecting the most suitable material out of which to construct a measuring rod. You will want it to be least responsive to changes in temperature, among other things).

''*Auri sacra fames!*'' [28] So exclaimed the Trojan hero *Aeneis* when he learned of the fate of his fellow prince *Polydorus*. The king of Troy, Priam, had sent Polydorus with a great weight of gold to the Thracian king asking for help to raise an army to relieve the besieged city. But when the Thracian king heard that the Trojans are not doing all that well against the Greeks, he took the gold by force and had Polydorus murdered in his sleep. "The accursed hunger for gold! To what do you not drive human hearts!"

Keynes gave currency to this quotation from Virgil to smear gold's good name. But as the original story shows, it is not the uses of gold but its *abuses* that ought to be castigated. All substances can be abused, gold is no exception.

It is an exercise in futility for the government to outlaw the trade and ownership of gold. No matter how many items the government may outlaw or confiscate, there will always remain a most marketable one that is ready to fill the shoes of gold.[29]

Chapter 8. Can Value be Measured?

According to von Mises values can be compared, but they cannot be measured. However, economic calculation plays an important role in his writings; in particular, think of his famous prediction made in the 1920's, that the Soviet economic system will sooner or later collapse. It has to because, unlike the capitalist system of production, it is lacking the possibility of economic calculation. All the means of production have been nationalised by the Soviets and there is no market for them. The captains of industry are totally in the dark with regard to possible losses due to the lack of market prices for the material factors of production that they must employ. The prediction of von Mises materialised less than 70 years later (some 15 years after he died). This was a most brilliant triumph for deductive economics. It even put the CIA to shame that certainly did not anticipate the collapse of the 'Evil Empire' in spite of its budget in the hundreds of millions of dollars, until the day before it happened.

The question arises: if values cannot be measured, how is economic calculation possible under capitalism? Apparently von Mises was far too dogmatic in assuming the impossibility of measuring value. This is all the more curious since Menger already in the 19th century solved the problem by establishing the measuring rod, a unit weight of gold, with which measuring value has become possible. Keep in mind that there is no objective equivalence in exchange, e.g., in exchanging a silver coin for a pair of shoes, all that is meant is that in the subjective judgement of somebody, the latter is valued at least as much. Von Mises was blinded by the Quantity Theory of Money. He refused to accept the fact that the marginal utility of gold was, in fact, a non-zero constant. Gold is the ideal material out of which the measuring rod of value can be fashioned. No wonder that devotees of the QTM demur. To their mind the value of gold, like the value of anything else, cannot be constant as it depends on available quantity. But if there is one lesson we must learn from Menger, it is the recognition that gold has become money not by historical accident, nor by its alleged scarcity, but because of the fact that gold is the most marketable substance we have. It took an evolution lasting for thousands of years for gold to reach that status. The process goes back to prehistoric times, well before writing was invented. People were hoarding gold [30] as it was the best means of the original accumulation of capital through which income could be converted into wealth and wealth into income, long before anyone thought of the exchange of wealth and income. Gold hoards had existed before gold became money. Lending and borrowing was unheard-of; individuals saved by hoarding gold, and drew on their savings by dishoarding (i.e., selling their gold piecemeal as the need arose). As the savings of an increasing population grew, the stocks-to-flows ratio for gold became a high multiple (at present variously estimated between 50 and 80, meaning that at the present rate of gold production it would take 50 to 80 years of output to duplicate existing stocks) while the ratio for all other goods (save silver) it is a small fraction. E.g., for copper it is about one-third (meaning that stockpiles do not exceed four months' mine output) because of the fast-declining marginal utility of copper that prevents large-scale accumulation.

There are far-reaching consequences. Gold continues to be mined in good times as well as in bad most economically, without any fear of a glut. According to von Mises it is nonsensical to talk about constant marginal utility because it would imply infinite demand. However, in saying this, von Mises had overlooked the existence of interest. Interest is a regulator of the demand for gold. It prevents demand from getting arbitrarily large. NASoE recognises the contact between gold and interest after John Fullarton first pointed it out in 1844 (cf. Chapter 15.) It has developed a comprehensive theory of gold, interest, capital accumulation, as well as of measuring value and forming prices without reference to supply/demand equilibrium. Note that these two concepts are indefinable in markets with speculator participation. Speculators could turn from buyers to sellers or from sellers to buyers on a moment's notice.

The gold-interest nexus is a great unifying idea in economics. Hence the value of gold and the purchasing power of gold must be carefully distinguished (see also p. 36 infra). Pieces of the jigsaw puzzle neatly fall into place. Once taken into account the objection is rebuffed. We conclude that value can be measured, and spreads are the valid measure of value, on which economic calculation rests.

Dogmatic clenching to the Quantity Theory of Money causes more harm than good. We should give full recognition to Menger's 'quality theory of money', placing the most marketable goods, gold and silver, into the centre. Their value has nothing to do with changing supply or demand. They owe their value not to their alleged scarcity, but to their supreme marketability.[31]

Chapter 9. Is Constant Marginal Utility Contradictory?

As already mentioned in Chapter 8, von Mises refused to acknowledge that gold has constant, nonzero marginal utility. His position is that constant marginal utility is contradictory as it implies infinite demand and infinitely high price. We respectfully disagree with von Mises. He went astray because he missed the point that interest payable for the privilege of using gold is a powerful deterrent, militating against an infinitely increasing high price. The tempering of the demand for gold by the requirement to pay interest for its use is obvious. Moreover, the rate of interest is variable and varies inversely with the propensity to save. The more people save, the greater amount of gold will be available for others with which to finance investments. Thus supply smoothly adjusts itself to demand: greater demand for gold calls out a greater supply through the mechanism of the variable interest rate.

John M. Keynes, the *enfant terrible* of economics asserted that not only gold but all other commodities also have their own rate of interest. In particular, he talks about the “wheat rate of interest”. This, of course, is pure bunk. It is meaningful to talk about interest only in relation to the commodity that commands constant nonzero marginal utility, that is, gold. If you want to borrow wheat, you just borrow gold and buy the wheat with the proceeds. There is no market for borrowing wheat. Keynes was fooled by the existence of futures markets for wheat. But these futures markets don’t let you borrow (consumable) wheat. What they do is just the opposite: they let you hedge your price risk if you have ‘borrowed’ wheat through the mechanism of borrowing gold. They help you restitute the ‘borrowed’ wheat on the best possible terms. As we can see from this example, only a commodity with stable value can be lent and borrowed on reasonable terms. In the previous Chapter we discussed why the value of gold is indeed constant. Gold is the very material out of which the measuring rod to measure value is fabricated. Devotees of the Quantity Theory of Money have a confused notion of marketability (as von Mises and von Hayek apparently did). Be that as it may, the idea that the value of gold varies is an oxymoron. The value of gold cannot vary any more than the length of a yardstick measured in terms of the yard can. If you reject gold as the material out of which the yardstick to measure value can be made, then you have to answer the question what is the true measure of value. No matter how you look at it, the only constant in economics must be derived from the idea of *maximum marketability*.

Quantity theorists and other detractors of gold argue that the value of gold is palpably variable as witnessed by the great historical episodes of gold dispersal and out of gold mines "hedging" their production. There were three such episodes: the sack of Persepolis by Alexander the Great in 330 B.C., the sack of Cusco by Pizzaro in 1534 A.D., and the sham demonetisation of gold by Richard Nixon in 1973. Each of these episodes was followed by price revolutions. E.g., the sack of Cusco was followed by a prolonged period of rising prices first in Spain (to where the looted gold was first shipped) lasting over a hundred years, then, in the rest of Europe, as gold (and silver) percolated down to other countries. The impression was that the value of gold fell. However, in each of these episodes the availability of consumer goods was greatly reduced in the wake of a spending orgy. We argue that price revolutions were always and everywhere the consequence of the scarcity of consumer goods, never that of an alleged abundance of gold. In the latest episode the world has experienced an unprecedented increase in prices, accompanied by a fall in the purchasing power of gold. This was partly the result of auctioning off US Treasury and IMF gold and, most notoriously, auctioning off half of the gold reserve of the Bank of England at record low prices at the end of the 20th century; and the sham demonetisation of gold and the propaganda accompanying it.

But, for the most part, the fall in the purchasing power of gold was the result of a spending spree arising out of abolishing compulsory gold reserves for banks to secure the dollar.

One has to distinguish between the value of gold and the purchasing power of gold. Since there is no other good the marketability of which is the same or greater than that of gold, the value of gold has not changed and will not change within the limits of our observation – in spite of great changes in the purchasing power of gold. We have to call attention to the glaring fact that in those periods when the purchasing power of gold was falling, such as the last decades of the 20th century, for example, the purchasing power of non-gold currencies was falling even more. Therefore it is no argument against the gold standard that sometimes the purchasing power of gold goes through a prolonged decline. There is no historical episode on record during which the purchasing power of paper currencies remained stable while that of gold was falling.[32] In each and every case the purchasing power of paper currencies *fell more*. Those fond of harping on the deficiencies of the gold standard, pointing to historical periods when the purchasing power of gold was falling, of course never mention this fact.

The fall in the purchasing power of gold apparently came to an end at the simultaneous turn of the century and millennium. As indicated by the ignominious failure of the gold mines "hedging" policy aided and abetted by central banks, gold is reasserting itself as the universal unit of value. We just have to put the idea to rest that the value of gold is subject to rising and falling as that of other substances.

Chapter 10. Is Paper Money a Present Good or a Future Good?

The bone of contention between von Mises and NASoE is the question posed in the title of this Chapter. According to von Mises, a gold certificate (a.k.a. 'yellowback') is just as much a present good as the gold coin which it promises to pay bearer on demand. As long as its maturity and security is not in question, the gold certificate can perform all the monetary functions that the gold coin can. In saying this, von Mises obliterates the difference between a promise and the object of a promise. He also ignores the fact that a gold certificate is listed in the asset column of the balance sheet of its owner; but unless it also appears in the liability column of the balance sheet of someone else, the gold certificate is worthless. For the gold coin there is no such limitation. Gold is the only asset that is not the liability of a third party. Consider the fact that, upon consolidating all balance sheets in the US (including that of the US Treasury) the value of gold *certificates* will evaporate. The value of gold *coins* will not.

Payment in gold coin is the ultimate settler of debt. No other method of payment will extinguish debt,[33] which is merely shifted from the debtor to the bank or, ultimately, to the US Treasury. It is a fable that the US Treasury can expand credit without limit, thanks to its ability to extend the maturity of its debt at will indefinitely. As the 'sovereign debt crisis' of the European governments most convincingly shows, government debt has its limits, too. Like private debt, it can be and is being abused. There is another crisis in the offing right now that has not yet hit the headlines: the sovereign debt crisis of the US government. This crisis is far more serious than other sovereign debt crises in Europe, already in the headlines (Triffin's Paradox).[34] When it bursts upon the scene, the world's monetary and payment system will unravel for reasons having to do with the fact that practically all central banks cover their note liabilities with U.S. government obligations.

Von Mises actually goes a lot farther than promoting gold certificates to the status of a present good. He promotes irredeemable paper money of every stripe in the same way. Not only is the yellowback a present good in his view, but so is the greenback and every other inconvertible paper money. In insisting that they, too, constitute present value von Mises contradicts himself. Elsewhere in his writings he eloquently and wittily says that only the government can work the miracle of taking a perfectly useful commodity, paper, sprinkle some ink on it thereby rendering the paper perfectly worthless.

There is no need to blot out the distinction between a present good and a future good. A gold coin is a present good; a gold certificate as well as any kind of fiat money is a future good (we hope so). According to the adage "there's many a slip between cup'n lip". On March 6, 1933, such a fatal slip occurred when President F. D. Roosevelt worked the miracle of turning an alleged present good, the 20 dollar greenback into a lump of butter of much less value. As the butter was exposed to the Sun, a meltdown of values both at home and abroad started. But the double eagle (20 dollar gold coin) was impervious to monetary mischief as well as the effect of the Sun. It was (and still is) acceptable in unlimited quantity at its original value abroad, despite presidential proclamations. True, at home it was not; but that was because of the strong arm of government. If you accepted it, you were going to jail. Napoleon and the glory of his empire is long gone, but the twenty-franc gold coin, also called Napoleon, is very much alive, and will be for a long time to come, regardless of the fortunes of Napoleon himself and that of his empire.

In Chapter 15 below we shall see that von Mises also is in error when he states that the gold *certificate* can perform all the monetary functions that the gold *coin* can. However, one function it definitely cannot perform. It cannot cast the protest vote against the suppression of the rate of interest by the government and banks. The error of von Mises is all the greater because the formation of the rate of interest cannot be understood without reference to the control people have over the floor of the rate of interest – by virtue of their right to refuse gold certificates and demand gold coins in selling their gold bond. Refuse they will because their bond still pays interest, however little, while the gold certificate does not.

The irredeemable paper dollar (F.R. note) of today is the result of a criminal conspiracy between the U.S. Treasury and the Federal Reserve System (Fed), popularly known as 'check-kiting', whereby they both issue liabilities for which they take no further responsibility whatsoever. The Treasury issues bonds, the Fed issues F.R. credit (namely, F.R. notes and F.R. deposits). In neither case is any meaningful provision for redemption made. The Treasury bond is ostensibly payable at maturity in F.R. credit. However, F.R. credit is created on the collateral security of the self-same Treasury bond.[35] In reality, therefore, it amounts to nothing more than silly prestidigitation at best. At worst, it is criminal defrauding of the people at home and abroad.

This raises the following question: by what valid reasoning can one justify the procedure of issuing liabilities which the issuer has neither the intention nor the means to honour? Check kiting is dealt with by the Criminal Code. We are here facing a most serious infraction of the Principle of No Double Standard.[36] Our monetary system is based on practices that would, if they were engaged in by private individuals or firms, land the perpetrators in jail. The government is telling its subjects: "*Do as I say, not as I do*". Is this an honourable position for a self-respecting government to take? Is the welfare of the American people and that of the people of the world in good hands of upright and law-abiding statesmen? Or, perchance, it is in the hands of crooks? [37]

If we are to believe von Mises, present goods can be created through check-kiting. Perhaps it was this favourable citation of von Mises, that "fiat money is a present good", that emboldened the authors of the paper dollar system to propose that counterfeit dollars are all right as long as they are issued through official channels and sanctioned by officials. Never mind that the officials have perjured themselves in the process – indeed, they are impostors, usurpers, or worse.

The question arises why the perpetrators of fiat money in the 20th century found it necessary to indulge in such a contorted process as check-kiting. They could have simply replaced F.R. notes by circulating T-bills. President Lincoln in the 19th century could get away with that in forcing the circulation of non-interest-bearing Treasury notes. Well, in forcing the circulation of greenbacks Lincoln had to suspend *habeas corpus*. He simply put people in jail if they failed to comply with his executive orders.

There is no need to suspend habeas corpus today in order to force the circulation of the irredeemable dollar (for the time being, anyway). This is a sad commentary on our educational system as it presently exists. In the 19th century people knew their Constitutional rights, they knew what the President could or could not do. Today they meekly accept any affront from the President concerning their property rights or any other right.

Chapter 11. The 100 Percent Gold Standard of Rothbard versus the Unadulterated Gold Standard

Murray Rothbard used the designation '100 percent gold standard' for what he said was the most desirable monetary system. The designation is disingenuous. If something is 100 percent, it must be good, mustn't it? Except that it is a pipe dream. It cannot be realised. Demand for money is swinging between widely different extremes, and gold coin circulation is far too rigid to be able to satisfy it. An expansion of demand (regularly occurring in the Christmas shopping season) would cause unwarranted price rises. A contraction of demand (regularly occurring during the first month of the year) would cause unwarranted price declines making the economy buckle under a deflationary strain. Likewise during harvest-time, the stock of circulating gold coins is unable to move the crop from the field to storage.

100 percent gold reserve banking is a pipe dream as well. Not only is it unrealisable; there is no need for it either. According to a famous adage of Adam Smith it is wasting precious resources. He called the use of real bills maturing into gold in bank reserves a 'waggon-way in the sky'. [38] There is no need to take land out of production as earthbound waggon-ways do. Real bills are the best earning assets the bank can have. If cash gold were used in every single exchange, then there would be a squeeze on the pool of circulating gold coins more urgently needed as a catalyst in facilitating capital accumulation. Traders along the supply-chain handling semi-finished consumer goods never insisted on cash settlement of their claims. Bills were drawn "91 days net" to allow plenty of time to collect the gold coin of the consumer to pay them.

The ideal monetary system is not Rothbard's so-called 100 percent gold standard. It is the unadulterated gold standard. Three of its features must be given prominence:

(1) the unconditional right of bearer to convert his gold bullion of the right quantity and quality into gold coins of the realm at the

Mint free of seigniorage charges, along with the unconditional right to hoard, melt or export the coins of the realm as the owner sees fit;

(2) the unconditional interdiction of borrowing short to lend long;

(3) the temporary monetary privileges extended to real bills.

The phrase "illicit interest arbitrage" catches the idea of borrowing short to lend long. Whereas arbitraging long-term to short-term funds along the yield curve is perfectly legitimate and unobjectionable, arbitrage in the opposite direction is illicit and it is to be dealt with by the Criminal Code for negligence of duties. It is useless to argue that selling bills in order to invest the proceeds in the bond market should be up to the discretion of the individual investor. When the bills expire, they must be replaced with new bills to keep the arbitrage unimpaired. However, bids on bills could evaporate in the meantime. This is exactly what happened to mortgage-backed securities in 2008. Bids for the mortgages backing bonds vanished, consequently, there was no market for the bonds either. The freedom of individuals to make contracts as they see fit is not absolute. Borrowing short to lend long, as all other 'something for nothing' schemes, undermine society. It is a prescription for disaster. In instances such as this the safety of social cooperation overrides individual freedom.[39]

Circulating gold and silver coins belong to the paraphernalia of the unadulterated gold standard. The right of the individual to convert standard quantity and quality of gold bullion into standard gold coins free of seigniorage charges must be enshrined in the Constitution (as it was, and still is, in the U.S.) Denial of this right by officials is unconstitutional and must be treated on a par with high treason.

Gold bonds issued by the government should, like any publicly traded bond, be subject to sinking fund provision. Principal and interest are payable in the gold coin of the realm. Politicians engineering a default on the public debt must not be able to escape prosecution after their term has expired.

The unadulterated gold standard must afford full protection against fraudulent default on commercial bills. Also called real bills, they are payable in gold coins upon maturity within 91 days or less. They are the best earning asset that a commercial bank can have. They are the most marketable instrument second only to the gold coin itself. Violation of the conditions to draw them (for example, making a false statement on the face of the bills, or redrawing them on left-over merchandise) must be made a criminal offence, on par with counterfeiting.

Real bills circulate spontaneously (cf. Chapter 14). If the banking system becomes insolvent and all banks close their doors, as it could happen in view of the present crisis, the production and distribution of consumer goods will not come to a sudden halt. They will be financed by real bills.

However, gold coins must be available to pay expiring real bills at maturity. Therefore the Mint must be open to the unlimited coinage of gold. Without gold coins the production and distribution of consumer goods may break down. This is our answer to those who try to disparage gold by crying: "You can't eat gold!" True, you can't eat gold; but without gold you may not be able to eat at all. Bills financing food production will not circulate unless they mature in gold. Gold coins must also be available to pay wages. Wage earners must have access to gold and silver coins in order to validate their choices in their capacity as consumers.

As a practical matter, gold coins cannot be made so small as to meet the requirements of the retail trade. The problem is solved by having the Mint strike subsidiary silver coins on Treasury account. These silver coins are not full-bodied, i.e., their face value is higher than their melt-down value (unlike the gold coin of the realm, which must be a full-bodied coin). However, the Treasury by law must have a 100 per cent gold reserve against subsidiary silver coins, and is under obligation to redeem them on demand in the gold coin. Payment in subsidiary coin is subject to a limit.

There must also be a limit on the use of paper currency in paying wages, by eliminating small denomination bank notes. It goes without saying that legal tender privileges of bank notes must be eliminated.

The unadulterated gold standard is more than simply a free market in money and credit. Some economists argue against limiting the individuals' right to make contracts as they see fit. They are woefully uninformed about the social harm done by credit expansion through peddling short-term funds as cover for long-term lending.

The recent (2012) plan of the Fed, dubbed 'Operation Twist', is a shameless attempt to make borrowing short to lend long appear legitimate and safe. The Fed is selling short-term debt from portfolio to buy long-term debt. The objective is to halve interest rates serially *ad libitum*. This effort is highly deflationary – although this is not recognised by the Fed – as falling interest rates always metastasise into falling prices.

Chapter 12. Menger and the Quantity Theory of Money

Mises built his entire theory of money and credit on the Quantity Theory of Money (QTM). He did say, though, that his was a 'modern' QTM in so far as it realised that there was a delay between the cause (increase in the money supply) and the effect (rising prices); hence those who could lay their hands on the newly created money first (e.g., people with government and bank connections such as special interest groups and various other pressure groups) would benefit at the expense of those who were last in line (e.g., pensioners). Yet this does not address the main fault of the QTM which is this: newly printed money can be spent not only on goods and services (causing prices and wages to increase), but on bonds as well (causing interest rates to fall). It is even conceivable that none of the newly printed money goes to pay for goods and services, but all of it goes to buy bonds. If that is the case, there will be no increase in the price of goods and services no matter how extreme the inflation may be. Instead, there will be deflation galore as the falling interest rate structure translates into a falling price structure and capital destruction. The contemporary experiment with unlimited inflation is a case in point. We have relatively little by way of price increases, but an alarming destruction of capital. The worst aspect of inflation (read: artificial increase in the money supply by the central bank) is that it creates a false euphoria of well-being and it helps governments to perpetuate their power while insidiously undermining capital preparing the ground for bankruptcies and huge unemployment, followed by breakdown of law and order.

In the spirit of Menger NASOE criticises von Mises for endorsing the QTM that at best is a clever mechanical metaphor, at worst, it is a thoroughly bad theory without redeeming features. It treats the world as if it was linear when, in effect, it is highly nonlinear. If we check the indexes of Menger's two most important books, the *Grundsätze* and the *Untersuchungen,* we shall not find one entry related to the QTM. Careful reading of other writings of Menger reveals that he never said anything of substance on the QTM either pro or con.

One should not jump to the conclusion that Menger had no opinion on the validity of QTM, and would be happy to let his students struggle with the problem. It is more likely that Menger was disturbed by the idea that the QTM made gold and silver appear more or less valuable according to changing supply. He firmly believed that gold's monetary role was due to its supreme marketability that had nothing to do with temporary changes in supply. He was alive to the fact that in terms of the ratio of stocks to annual flows gold is far from being scarce: it is more abundant than any other commodity the marginal utility of which declines faster (thus preventing a large build-up of large hoards). The value of gold (and silver) is not determined by quantity; it is determined by marketability. The powerful concept of marketability is the living denial of the QTM: quality pitted against quantity. If the purchasing medium is made of the material of the highest quality (read: of the most saleable and the most hoardable good), then its value is constant, regardless of its 'purchasing power'. We simply don't have any other standard to gage the stability of value.

It is very probable that Menger wanted to develop his theory of interest in a planned second edition of *Grundsätze* on which he was working during the last decade of his life, and he saved his criticism of the QTM for this work. Unfortunately he died before he could do it, and in this sense his opus remains incomplete.

Quantity theorists habitually conjure up the bogey man of gold hoarding in an effort to refute the claim that the value of gold is not more variable than the length of the yard in terms of the same yard is. They argue that gold hoarding makes gold scarce, causing prices to fall. Deflation follows. The truth of the matter however, is that talking about gold hoarding makes sense only if we also consider gold dishoarding in the context of the mechanism of the formation of the rate of interest. Gold hoarding is a protest vote: a warning signal that the government and the banks have gone too far in pushing the rate of interest lower. The marginal bondholder is protesting the violation of his time preference. He sells his overpriced bond, keeping the proceeds in gold coins. Should the government and the banks heed the warning and rein in the credit expansion, the public will dishoard gold.

At any rate, if the government wants to eliminate gold hoarding, there is a very simple way to do it. It should allow the interest rate to return to its *natural rate,* namely, the level of marginal time preference. The marginal bondholder will react by releasing his hoarded gold. He will buy his bond back at a profit. What he is in fact doing is a profitable arbitrage operation between the bond market and the gold market. This arbitrage is very effective: it keeps the government and the banks on a short leash. The profitability of this arbitrage is the guarantee that the government will pursue the enlightened policy of "hands off" as far as the rate of interest is concerned. This is how God ordained the world. The rate of interest and its variation is no business of the government. It is the business of the people who retain their control through increasing or decreasing their outright possession of gold.

All economists have missed this essential role of gold in the formation of the interest rate with the exception of John Fullarton. (1780? –1849) He pointed out the connection between gold hoarding and the suppression in the rate of interest in his book *On the Regulation of Currencies,*[40] first published in 1844. Von Mises dismissed the Fullarton Effect with a contemptuous remark calling it *Deus ex machina* ("God crawling out of the woodwork"). For more on this, see Chapter 15 *infra.*

This epitaph turned out to be more apt than von Mises intended. The role that gold is supposed to play in the economy to keep it on an even keel was forcibly overruled by the government. By eliminating gold from the monetary system, conceited men eliminated God from economics as well. But God is punishing men for their utter conceitedness, as he had punished the people of the Old Testament for theirs. The contemporary Tower of Babel is made of debt as manifested by the tower of derivatives. The mindless experiment will end the same way. According to the Bible, God confused the language of the builders of the Tower of Babel that was supposed to reach the sky. After God confused their language they could no longer communicate with one another. The Tower of Babel collapsed and buried its conceited builders under the rubble. In the contemporary episode God is confusing the currencies of the builders of the debt tower. This tower is also doomed. Lamentably, the effect will not be confined to one city. The collapse of the Debt Tower will bury virtually all the inhabitants of the globe under the rubble – punishment for the conceit of our leaders in trying to play God. This raises the question: how is it that our leaders did not see the disaster into which they were leading the people? The answer is: the Quantity Theory of Money has blurred their vision.

Chapter 13. The Wisdom of Adam Smith

Mainstream Austrian Economics treats Adam Smith as one might treat a poor relative. His name is virtually never mentioned, except in the context of the mistake he made in connection with the theory of value. As is well-known, Adam Smith embraced the ancient fallacy that the value of a product was proportional with the socially necessary amount of human labour going into its production. (Karl Marx' system was also based on the same fallacy.) But what the American Austrians really cannot forgive Adam Smith is the fathering of the Real Bills Doctrine. It is an anathema for them since it refutes the Quantity Theory of Money (QTM), the Holy Grail of Austrian monetary theory.

It is ironical that mainstream Austrians, rightly, combat positivism – except that they embrace the QTM, a paramount example of positivist thinking and barren theorising. By contrast, Adam Smith's Real Bills Doctrine is a paragon of theorising while refusing to fall into the trap of positivism. It remains faithful to reality.

It is a fact that real bills drawn on maturing semi-finished goods did circulate spontaneously in Lancashire before the Bank of England opened its branch office in Manchester, as observed by von Mises himself. It is also a fact that real bill circulation did not give occasion to price rises. The bill expired simultaneously with the sale of merchandise to the ultimate consumer, on which it had been drawn. At no point in time did bill circulation exceed the quantity of finished and semi-finished goods on the way to the consumer. What these bills did was to provide "bridge-financing" in moving semi-finished goods, bringing them one step closer to the ultimate consumer.

We owe the example of the spinner-weaver supply chain leading to the ultimate consumer of cloth to von Mises himself. He observed that the bill drawn on the yarn delivered to the weaver was acceptable in payment to the suppliers of the spinner. To insist that the weaver pay in gold coin for the yarn shipped by the spinner, along with the spinner also paying in gold coin for the bale of wool to the wool merchant, is unrealistic in the extreme. A consistent execution of such a program would put an intolerable squeeze on the pool of circulating gold coins and would ultimately lead to the collapse of the gold standard.

Adam Smith did see this. Furthermore, he realised that there was simply no need for paying gold at the time of delivery of semi-finished goods by one producer to the next. As a matter of merchant custom traders like the spinner and the weaver routinely accepted properly drafted and endorsed bills in payment for the consignment of yarn and cloth. They were happy to wait patiently for their share of the gold coin that was to be released by the ultimate consumer, and would reach them in good time, at any rate no more than 91 days, as their predecessors have for hundreds of years before them.

Adam Smith's famous metaphor about the "waggon-way in the sky" in the *Wealth of Nations* is most convincing. Gold has a far more important role to play in the economy than being merely a purchasing medium, facilitating the payment of the spinner for yarn delivered which, in any case, can be made with self-liquidating credit. By contrast, gold is indispensable in financing capital accumulation and capital deployment. If you wanted to replace gold in this capacity by drawing bills, and tried to put these bills into circulation, you would be disappointed and rebuffed. Traders wouldn't touch your bill with a ten-foot pole. There would be no bid for them. Believe me, it has been tried any number of times, and failed in every instance. Waggon-way in the sky works only for consumer goods in most urgent demand, and it utterly fails to work for capital goods for which amortisation may take years. The marketability of real bills is way higher than that of the best corporate bond, or that of Treasury bonds, even Treasury bills for that matter. We only have to look at the bid/asked spread at which they are traded. A real bill can be bought and sold back-to-back with virtually no loss. That's why real bills are the best earning asset commercial banks can have to cover their sight liabilities. A run on the bank can be successfully beaten back by liquidating the bank's portfolio of real bills.

Real bills were in very high demand indeed, far beyond the needs of trade in semi-finished consumer goods. Anyone in need to assemble a large sum of money, whether to purchase a house or whether to retire a bond issue, would do it by assembling a portfolio of maturing real bills. Von Mises does not appear to have realised that. In the 19th century every time a house was sold, the buyer never paid for his purchase by surrendering gold coins. He paid for it by surrendering real bills maturing (into gold coins) on the day the sale was to be consummated. Nor were corporate bonds (which typically carried a gold clause) retired at maturity by handing over a sack of gold coins to the bondholder. They were retired through handing over a portfolio of real bills which the corporation assembled over a period of time in such a way that the maturity of the bills should dove-tail with that of the bond.

Chapter 14. Spontaneity of Real Bill Circulation

All the arguments against the Real Bills Doctrine and the Banking School enumerated by von Mises refers to banks that use (abuse) real bills in their portfolio of assets serving as collateral against bank loans to businesses. While he does not deny that real bills could circulate spontaneously, von Mises does not consider spontaneous real bill circulation as a phenomenon worthy of closer attention. However, a proper analysis of Adam Smith's Real Bills Doctrine should put the problem in a correct setting, including a look at a hypothetical economy where banks simply do not exist.

In such an economy real bills would circulate as medium of exchange on their own wings and under their own steam. Their circulation would be entirely spontaneous. The bill market would be the supreme judge in deciding which bills it would discount and which ones it would refuse to discount. Very little, if any regulation is needed provided that the bill market is transparent. The market is ingenious enough to find its means of exchange even in the complete absence of commercial banks. In many ways such an absence might even be salutary. Banks withdraw the lion's share of real bills from the public domain. They make them private documents in bank portfolios. The bill market can no longer be overseen by the public. That gives rise, nay, invites, collusion. 'Pig-on-pork' style bills will crop up in violation of the rules. In the absence of banks such bills could not be sheltered from public scrutiny. The bill market would spot them and refuse to discount them before they could do much harm. Furthermore, expiring bills on unsold merchandise could be quietly 'rolled over' by your friendly banker in violation of the rules. This is the main danger of allowing banks to treat bills in their portfolio as privileged documents. The public should have the right to know what's going on. It should have the final say in which bills should be refused discounting. Banks should have been forbidden to roll over expiring bills on leftover merchandise in collusion with their favoured clients.

The advent of commercial banks and their practice of withdrawing spontaneously circulating bills from the market was motivated by the convenience of bank notes as a proxy for the real bill. Bank notes came in standard denomination. No expiry date was specified to watch. The name-recognition of the bank was superior to that of the firm on which the real bill was drawn. In fact, the convenience that the bank note afforded was such that people were willing to forgo the discount that would be theirs otherwise. They also gave up their right to oversee that the banks do actually withdraw the right amount of bank notes from circulation every time the underlying real bill matured. The temptation on banks was too great to put such bank notes back in circulation for other purposes, such as loans on personal consumption or on capital projects, a practice that was against the rules.

All in all, the record of commercial banks and the role they have played in the bill market is mixed. One can say that the banks did not deserve the trust that was accorded to them. They should have been kept on short leash. Their portfolio of maturing real bills should have been open to public scrutiny. Bank supervision should have been much tighter, fines on banks violating the rules higher. The public should have been made cognisant of bank violations, especially when they have been recurring. In particular, bank inspectors should have blown the whistle every time when they saw a bank paying out bank notes illegally, rather than withdrawing them from circulation upon the expiration of the underlying real bill.

By now bank abuses have gone so far that the entire banking system has become insolvent and could collapse at any time. If that happens, that will not be the end of the world. As a matter of fact, the world can live without banks. Spontaneous real bill circulation can take over financing the production and distribution of consumer goods in most urgent demand.

Chapter 15. The Fullarton Effect

The concept of marginal time preference originates with the Scottish economist John Fullarton (1780 – 1849) who in his book On the Regulation of Currencies, first published in 1844, pointed out the causal nexus between the suppression of interest by banks and gold hoarding that came to be known as the Fullarton Effect. Von Mises ridiculed the Fullarton Effect and called it Deus ex machina. Von Mises was wrong. Gold hoarding is the corner stone of the theory of interest, marking the level below which neither the government nor the banks are able to push the rate of interest without further serious consequences.

In Chapter 10 above we tackled the problem whether a gold certificate (yellowback) is a present good or, as common sense may suggest, whether it is a future good. We came to the conclusion that, like any promise to deliver a commodity in the future, a gold certificate is also a future good. Von Mises made a major mistake in classifying it (as well as classifying all irredeemable currency) a present good. To the best of my knowledge his judgment has not been challenged by other authors, nor was his summary dismissal of the Fullarton Effect criticised.

Let us now see the detailed argument why von Mises is in error when he suggests that the gold certificate can also perform all the monetary functions that the gold coin can. One function it definitely cannot perform. Consider the marginal bondholder's reaction to the suppression of the rate of interest below his time preference rate (a.k.a. the rate of marginal time preference) by the banking system. He will sell his overpriced gold bond in protest and keep the proceeds in gold coin, until the banks stop suppressing the rate of interest and allow it to increase and reach its natural level. At that point the marginal bondholder will repurchase his bond at a lower price. Without this arbitrage between the bond market and the gold market the formation of the rate of interest cannot be understood. At any rate, the marginal bondholder would refuse to take a gold certificate in exchange for his bond. It would make his protest nonsensical. He would be jumping from the frying pan into the fire. His action would be counterproductive: the bond does pay interest, however little, while the gold certificate does not pay any. This is one function that the gold certificate cannot perform but the gold coin can: to cast the protest vote against the banks' suppression of the rate of interest below the rate of marginal time preference. And a very important function it is.

Gold hoarding is not an aberration as some authors suggest. Keynes even said that the study of the phenomenon is not the task of the economist. It is, rather, the task of the psychopathologist. The truth is, however, that gold hoarding has a central role to play in the formation of the rate of interest. It is the manifestation of a protest vote against the loose credit policies of the banks, and against government profligacy. So much for Keynes' understanding of interest and of psychopathology.

Von Mises was obsessed with the demand for money. Strictly speaking there is no such a thing. There is demand for gold arising out of the Fullarton Effect. Gold hoarding is the only effective way to protest the banks' suppression of the rate of interest. The rest of what von Mises subsumes under the heading 'demand for money' is really demand for consumer goods. But according to the Real Bills doctrine of Adam Smith, if the demand is sufficiently urgent, bills will be drawn and discounted to finance the production and distribution of consumer (first order) goods. Demand for higher order goods will cause the rate of interest to rise, which will make the marginal bondholder dishoard gold.

Chapter 16. The Rate of Interest and the Marginal Productivity of Capital

As mentioned in Chapter 4, according to von Mises the rate of interest, unlike prices, is not the product of a market process. He postulates time preference that determines what he calls 'originary interest'. In this view the market rate is a modification of the rate derived from originary interest – taking other factors such as risk of default into account. We have pointed out that originary interest is a phantom: it is trying to second guess what someone will think or do in the future.

We have also dealt with the question how the rate of interest manifests itself in the first place. How can one find out what the rate of interest at any moment is? Asking the neighbouring pawnshop manager is not good enough. We get a better idea if we go to the bond market and get a quotation on the bond price. The inverse relationship between the rate of interest and the bond price can be compared to a see-saw: while the rate of interest goes up, the bond price comes down and vice-versa.[41] The bond market is huge; lending and borrowing outside of the bond market is minuscule in comparison, suggesting that the rate of interest manifests itself through the bond price.

But the main reason why we at NASoE reject von Mises' theory of interest is his categorical refusal to admit that the productivity of capital has anything to do with the rate of interest. As mentioned in Chapter 3, this flies in the face of facts. When the rate of interest goes up, a lot of productive capital becomes submarginal. The marginal entrepreneur sells his plant and equipments (or at least stops maintaining them). He puts the proceeds and his savings on capital maintenance into bonds which are cheap now and offer a high yield. Conversely, if the rate of interest comes down, the marginal entrepreneur sells his bonds at a profit, buys back his plant and equipments and reboots capital maintenance. He is doing arbitrage between the bond market and the capital goods market. Without explicitly recognising this arbitrage (along with the arbitrage of the marginal bondholder between the bond market and the gold market) it is not possible to understand interest. Von Mises is wrong: the formation of the rate of interest is the result of market processes, very much like the formation of prices as described by the disequilibrium theory of price formation.

The theory of interest has a long and checkered history, mainly due to the original sin of Aristotle. He postulated, mistakenly, that taking and paying interest is against natural law because gold, an inert matter, unlike cattle and sheep (that used to serve as money in prehistoric times), does not beget gold. After Christianity became the dominant religion, St. Thomas of Aquinas (1225 – 1274) in his *Summa Theologiae* transplanted the pagan philosophy of Aristotle into Christian dogma. Taking and paying interest has become a cardinal sin and it was not until the 19th century that usury was redefined and proscription against interest was lifted by the Catholic Church. To a large extent this was done in response to prompting from Protestant philosophers.

The theory of interest is still in a backward state. The fratricidal war between factions of Austrian economists, one subscribing to the productivity theory and the other to the time preference theory of interest, still continues. NASoE is the first to suggest that it is possible, in the spirit of Carl Menger, to find a synthesis between the positions of the two factions. This depends on starting with a new formulation of the definition of the rate of interest. We have given this new definition in Chapter 4: The current rate of interest is that rate at which the coupons (representing interest payments without amortisation) plus the repayment of the principal sum at maturity amortise the market value (as opposed to the face value) of the bond. The bond market, just as the market for commodities, quotes bid and asked prices. These determine the ceiling and the floor (in this order!) of the range in which the rate of interest may move. [*Ed. See figure 3B, 4 and 5 pp. 63 & 68*]. As in the case of commodities, the forces responsible for the formation of the bid and asked price are entirely different, and call for separate analyses. In particular, the floor of the rate of interest is determined by marginal time preference (time preference of the marginal bondholder). The ceiling, on the other hand, is determined by the marginal productivity of capital (that is, the productivity of the marginal capital good). In this way the fratricidal war can have a happy end. In no event is the Fed in a position to determine the rate of interest. In 1937 the Board of Governors of the Federal Reserve System still maintained that it has no way to control the rate of interest, except for exercising influence over the shortest of short rates at which member banks borrow from one another overnight (the federal funds rate).

It is clear that a *coup d'état*, or several of them, took place between 1937 and now. Under each, unelected Federal Reserve officials were allowed by elected officials to grab more and more power over the interest rate structure stealthily. As a result by now the Fed controls the entire spectrum of interest rates on the yield curve. In this F.R. officials were greatly helped by academic economists who failed to point out to the public the usurpation of power involved, and the harm done thereby.

Mainstream Austrian economists were no exception. They were barking up on the wrong tree. (Another wrong tree is the chimera of 'fractional' reserve banking.) They summarily dismiss real bills maturing into gold coins as proper reserves held against bank notes. However, in doing so post-Mises Austrians ignore the real problem of seasonal variations in the demand for credit (such as during the harvest season). The financial system needs an elastic supply of credit. Real bills tide and ebb together with the volume of trade in consumer goods.

In charging that the F.R. Act of 1913 was unconstitutional, the post-Mises Austrians wash their hands and abdicate their responsibility to point out how the Act has been constantly violated from the start by the legislative, executive and judicial branches of government. All Fed and Treasury officials are impostors. They are guilty of a conspiracy to create money illegally and unconstitutionally through check-kiting. They pontificate what the rate of interest should be. The corruption of the U.S. and the world's monetary system could not be more complete. The only explanation for this sad state of affairs which the mainstream Austrian economists are able to offer is a faulty one, namely, that the Federal Reserve Act of 1913 was enacted in violation of the U.S. Constitution. They failed to examine the question whether the F.R. Act of 1913, before any amendment, was indeed constitutional, but it was corrupted piecemeal from day one on, first covertly and then, after the conspirators discovered that they can get away with violating the Constitution, overtly as well. The precise story of how the rate of interest in the world was corrupted must be told. Unfortunately, it is not possible to do that on the basis of von Mises' theory of interest which flatly denies that the rate of interest is the outcome of a market process. The corruption of the rate of interest has been accomplished through the corruption of the bond market. Is a greater corruption possible than a government selling unlimited amounts of bonds to the saving public (widows and orphans included) which it has neither the means nor the intention to redeem?

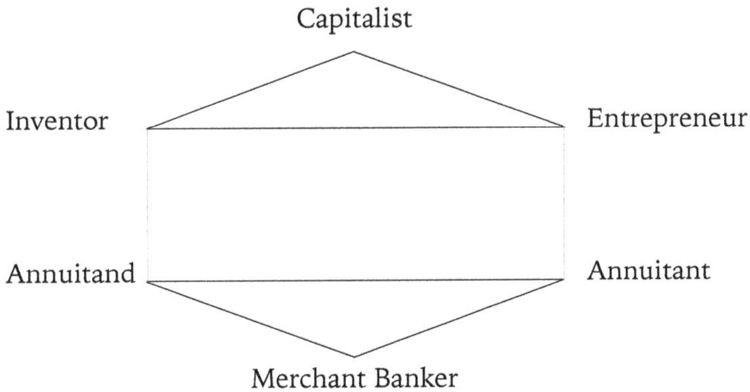

Figure 3 A The six roles in the Hexagonal Model of Capital and Interest Rate Formation.

Video demonstration on the formation of interest rates, available on https://www.youtube.com/watch?v=YN1vMdx-GiQ

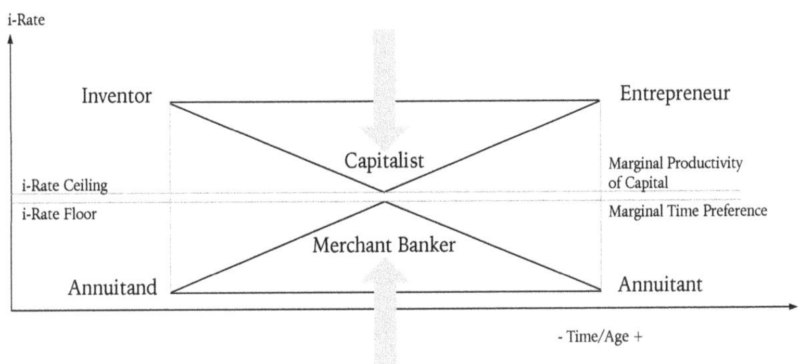

Figure 3 B All six roles in synergy to determine i-rates (floor and ceiling) under assumption of an unadulterated circulating gold coin standard.

Chapter 17. Gold and Interest

The greatest failure of Mainstream Austrian Economics is that it has missed the point of contact between gold and interest. Gold is held in high esteem because of its unusual physical and chemical properties and its alleged scarcity – not because gold is the cornerstone of the majestic building of the theory of interest, an idea inspired by the work of Carl Menger. Menger never published a comprehensive theory of interest. This does not mean that he thought the problem of interest could safely be left for the Historical School to study, or that deductive economics has nothing to add to the bare historical facts. Apparently Menger withheld whatever he had to say on the matter, and saved it for a long-planned second edition of his great work, The Principles of Economics on which he was working during the last decade of his life together with his son, Karl Menger (junior). To the eternal loss of the science of economics, Carl Menger (senior) died before his theory of interest could be completed. One can only guess what it would have looked like had he lived long enough to complete it.

The best we can do under these circumstances is to reconstruct it from other ideas of Menger. Starting with his seminal idea of the bid/asked spread we isolate the idea 'marketability in the small' or 'hoardability', the counterpart of 'marketability in the large' or 'saleability' – Menger's original idea, *Absatzfähigkeit*. In talking about hoarding we must also talk about its complement 'dishoarding'. The dichotomy hoarding / dishoarding suggests that the 'original accumulation of capital' depended on the conversion of income into wealth through hoarding the most hoardable goods (gold and silver). When the need arose, hoarded wealth was converted back into income through dishoarding.

Later it was realised that the time-consuming and wasteful way of direct conversion can substantially be shortened and improved by passing to indirect conversion, that is, the exchange of income and wealth. Interest now appears as the increase in the efficiency of conversion due to introducing exchange. Zero interest means zero exchange.[42] But as we have seen in Chapter 16, interest could never go to zero. The economising individual would walk away from exchange and fall back on hoarding before that happened. The bargaining powers of participants in the exchange of income and wealth are not symmetric. Veto power belongs to the provider of credit.

Needless to say the process of passing from direct to indirect conversion of wealth and income had to go hand-in-hand with the development of the legal framework. Indirect conversion would break down in the absence of legal protection of contract and security of exchange. The process was greatly hindered by the canonical and secular prohibition on interest taking and paying, due to a mistaken idea of Aristotle, namely, the idea that interest contradicts natural law as long as an inert material, rather than livestock such as cattle or sheep was used as money.

A perfectly legal bond market, where marketable bonds could be traded freely and the rate of interest could be quoted openly arrived only in the 19th century, after all canonical and secular prohibition against interest taking and paying was lifted. We must cut through this maze of legal morass to establish the fact that the definition of interest must be given in terms of the bond price as quoted in a widely traded bond market. Exchanging income and wealth cannot be made subject to duress.

After millennia of fruitless debates on usury it was not surprising that economists of the 20th century were using the wrong definition of interest. The correct definition (first mentioned in Chapter 4 above) should refer to the bond price as it is formed in the bond market: the prevailing rate of interest is that rate at which the coupons of the gold bond, representing interest payments (without amortisation), plus the lump-sum payment of the bond's face value at maturity amortise the market price of the bond. Note that the market price of the gold bond may deviate from its face value upwards as well as downwards. It is not an abnormal condition (as the uninitiated may think) if the price of the bond is quoted above face value. All it means is that the market rate of interest has fallen and, accordingly, the value of income represented by the bond – a fixed income security – has increased. Keep in mind that the market value of the gold bond and the market rate of interest always move in the opposite direction. The market value of the bond coincides with its face value only in the exceptional case when the market rate of interest coincides with the coupon rate of the bond.

Alternatively, we may consider participation in the equity market as an exchange of income for wealth, and vice versa. A company of people bringing their equity to the exchange forms an exchange of income for wealth, as does the bringing to market of a bond. The discovery of the rate of interest from the bond price, as described above, is analogous to the discovery of the return on equity.

Self-respecting governments should never consider issuing anything but gold bonds, with principal and interest payable in the gold coin of the realm. The bond's value should be protected by a sinking fund. The manager of the sinking fund would step in and buy every time the market quotation for the bond falls. Throughout history it was considered most reprehensible if a government diluted the gold coin of the realm to get out of debt on the cheap. Not just because of the prevailing moral imperative; but also on the strength of the principle of not tolerating double standards in jurisprudence. The government could not unilaterally exempt itself from its obligations any more than the individual citizen could. The same law governed dealings between citizens and the government and those between citizens. A citizen could take the government to court for breach of contract just as he could take a fellow citizen.

The days are long since past when the government felt itself inconvenienced by the Constitution, or moral principles for that matter. After throwing off its golden shackles stealthily and piecemeal in the 20th century the government could manipulate the money supply and the rate of interest as it saw fit in the 21st.

The government looks at its subjects as the farmer looks at his beasts of burden. Invisible slavery has been reinvented through exiling gold from the monetary system.

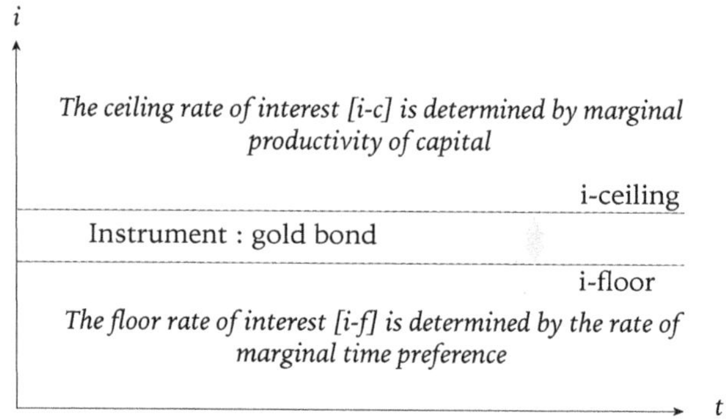

Figure 4

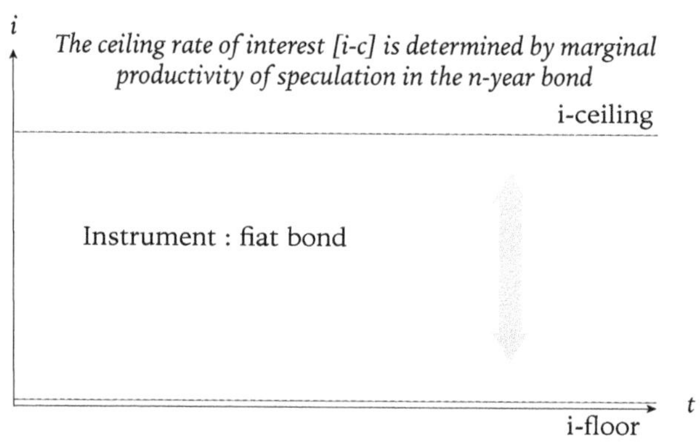

Figure 5

Chapter 18. The Discount Rate and the Marginal Productivity of Social Circulating Capital

In this Chapter we shall develop a theory of the retail trade to show how retailing differs from other markets, a point missed by mainstream Austrian economics. There are important differences due to the fact that items sold retail are destined to disappear in consumption. In all other markets people buy in order to sell (typically, they buy the higher-order good and sell the lower order good). Our effort can also be described as an extension of the Method of Marginalism to Adam Smith's Real Bills Doctrine.

This will put the theory of discount in a novel light showing that von Mises made a mistake when he blotted out the difference between the discount rate and the rate of interest. It is imperative to keep the two separate. Their sources and nature are entirely different. They play quite different roles in the economy. The rate of interest is the mirror image of the propensity to save; the discount rate is the mirror image of the propensity to consume - to borrow the felicitous phrases of Keynes. The two vary independently of one another: they could move in the same or in opposite directions. There is one critical interdiction: the rate of interest must not be lower than the discount rate. Pushing it below is the worst instance of illicit interest arbitrage. Yet the temptation is ever present for the banks to borrow short-term funds (i.e., selling bills in the bill market) and peddle the proceeds as long-term funds available for capital investments (i.e., buying bonds in the bond market). The banks pocket illicit risk-free profits in the process. The consequence is panic in the money-market as manifested by the inversion of the yield curve, causing widespread losses all around.

We owe the concept of social circulating capital (SCC) to Adam Smith. It is the flow of maturing consumer goods moving apace to the ultimate consumer paying with gold coins for the purchase. The retail merchant (a.k.a. shopkeeper) stocks his shelf with items belonging to the SCC. It is easy to see that not all items move with the same velocity: some (e.g., bread) are in more urgent demand than others (e.g., spices). We can talk about the productivity of each individual item in the SCC. It is just the retail markup divided by the average length of its sojourn on the shelf. We can now rank items belonging to the SCC according to productivity. A critical role is played by the marginal item of the social circulating capital, i.e., the first item that the marginal shopkeeper will eliminate from the shelf (will not reorder it) when its productivity declines in response to declining consumer interest. The marginal shopkeeper is the first to react to a change in the propensity to consume. The productivity of the marginal item is called the marginal productivity of social circulating capital.

The marginal productivity of SCC is instrumental in determining the size of the SCC. Increasing marginal productivity means that the shopkeeper eliminates the marginal item from his shelf in response to a lethargic consumer demand when the propensity to consume declines. Conversely, decreasing marginal productivity means that the shopkeeper will display a new marginal item on his shelf to allow the consumers to choose from a greater variety of goods. This happens when consumer buying is buoyant, when the propensity to consume grows. Thus the size of the SCC varies inversely with its marginal productivity.

The Law of Retail Trade asserts that the marginal productivity of the social circulating capital is equal to the discount rate. In Chapter 19 we shall discuss how the discount rate emerges when the shopkeeper, his till being flush with gold coins, decides to prepay his bill drawn by the wholesaler upon delivery of supplies. Prepay he will but only for a consideration. He insists on getting a discount on the face value of the bill. This is how the discount earns its name. Naturally, the discount is proportional to the number of days remaining to maturity. The proportionality factor is called the discount rate. We have seen that it varies inversely with the propensity to consume: the discount rate is lower when the consumer is in a buoyant mood; it is higher when he is tight-fisted. We shouldn't be fooled by the formal similarity between the discount rate and the rate of interest. They are both related to credit transactions, but in the case of the former the credit is self-liquidating. It is liquidated with the gold coin released by the consumer in purchasing the consumer good.

The important thing to note is that, in effect, the marginal shopkeeper is doing arbitrage between the bill market and the consumer goods market. His guiding star is the discount rate. A rise in the discount rate tells him that it is time for retrenchment. The consumer is going to cut spending. The marginal shopkeeper responds by eliminating the marginal item from his shelf. He will not reorder it. But he will not leave the resulting savings idle. He goes into the bill market and will buy bills drawn on other shopkeepers who are, at least for the moment, working with higher productivity. Conversely, a fall in the discount rate tells the marginal shopkeeper that the consumer is now ready to resume spending. He responds by ordering new (up to now submarginal) merchandise and paying for them by selling bills from portfolio. He then displays the new items on his shelf so that the consumer will be able to select from a greater variety of goods. There cannot be a discrepancy between the marginal productivity of the SCC and the discount rate. For if the latter were higher, then the marginal shopkeeper would remove the marginal item from the shelf and put the savings into real bills. If it were lower, then he would sell some of the real bills from portfolio and use the proceeds to display a greater variety of merchandise on his shelf. It is conceivable that the discount rate goes to zero. In that case the marginal shopkeeper is a curb side vendor displaying his wares on the sidewalk, possibly also after nightfall.

It should be abundantly clear that the funds turned over in the bill market are in no sense derived from savings and the discount rate has nothing whatsoever to do with the rate of interest. It is preposterous to assume that the wholesale merchant extends a loan to the retail merchant when replenishing the latter's stock of consumer goods; or that the producer of $(n + 1)^{th}$ order goods extends a loan to the producer of nth order goods when he delivers supplies on credit. The source of this credit (a.k.a. self-liquidating credit) is not savings but consumption. The scholastic fathers made a clear distinction between lending and discounting in the 15th century. They went to Rome to convince the pope that there was no usury involved in discounting a real bill. Can we afford to be more backward than these early but brilliant pioneers of economic science were?

Chapter 19. Gold and Discount

According to von Mises zero interest is not possible. Since the rate of interest varies inversely with the propensity to save, zero interest would imply infinite saving and zero consumption. People would save even the smallest morsel of food. This is clearly impossible. Without eating people would die. Von Mises was correct. The rate of interest can get halved any number of times; it would still be positive. It would never go to zero.

Von Mises failed to make a distinction between interest and discount. This was a most serious omission with far-reaching consequences. The sources and the nature of the two are entirely different. Interest varies inversely with the propensity to save. Discount varies inversely with the propensity to consume. Zero discount rate implies no saving. It means that people consume everything consumable they can lay their hands on. They behave as if there was no tomorrow. They would forgo capital accumulation and maintenance. Not only is this behaviour far from being impossible; it actually happened at the end of the first millennium when people were expecting doomsday to take place on January 1, 1001. It is also happening here and now, as manifested by the self-destructive behaviour of governments, following Keynes, foolishly assuming that in the aggregate one can consume now and save later. The results are only now begin to show up: the increase of private and public debt beyond any limit.

Very briefly we shall review here the rise of discount. It arose in the first place when the wholesale merchant delivered supplies to the retail merchant and billed him. The bill stated on its face: "91 days net". This meant that, following merchant custom, payment was not due immediately. It was due in 91 days, or 13 weeks, or 3 months. By the end of quarter the consumer good more closely described on the face of the bill will have been sold, and the bill could be paid in gold coins released by the consumers. The point is that with the change of the seasons of the year the type of merchandise in greatest consumer demand also changes. If merchandise could not be sold in

91 days, there is little chance to sell it in 273 = 3 x 91 days, before the same season of the year comes around again. However, the retail merchant has reserved the right of prepaying his bills. Discount (off the face value of the real bill) arises as the retail merchant's till is flush with gold coins and he exercises his right to prepay the bills drawn on him by the wholesale merchant.

It is a grave error to assume that the arrangement between the wholesaler and the retailer constitutes a loan. The credit was the retailer's for the taking. However, should he have the cash in the till, it was his privilege to prepay the bill at the time of delivery or at any other time before maturity. Naturally, he would do it only for a consideration. He would prepay the bill if there was an incentive in the form of a discount. Upon prepayment the wholesale merchant would discount the face value of the bill by the number of days remaining to maturity at the prevailing discount rate. As already mentioned, the discount rate depends on the propensity to consume. The relationship is inverse: the higher the propensity, the lower is the discount rate. Conversely, the lower the propensity to consume, the higher is the discount rate. If business is brisk, then the retailer expects to sell out the inventory faster. Accordingly, he is willing to accept a smaller discount. But when business is lethargic, the clearing his shelves of merchandise will take longer, raising the spectre that some of the goods would be still unsold on the day the bill matures. Because of this the wholesale merchant will be reluctant to grant the same, let alone a smaller, discount to the retailer.

Clearly, the origin of discount has nothing to do with that of interest. A separate analysis is needed in order to clarify the nature and the origin of either. Von Mises failed to see this and, as a consequence, his theory of interest is erroneous.

Let us examine the two extreme cases of the discount rate that could arise. When the propensity to consume is low (consumer demand is lethargic), the wholesale merchant will insist on a higher discount rate to reflect the prospect that the retail merchant will not be able to clear his shelves of merchandise in 91 days and the collection on the bill may face snags. In the other extreme case where the propensity to consume is most buoyant. Then the discount rate is falling. It could go all the way to zero (mark that the rate of interest could not). Vendors display their wares on the sidewalk at every street corner, even at night if need be. People quit low-paying jobs as they could earn more in selling goods that previously were only available in specialty shops. High propensity to consume and low propensity to save are not mutually exclusive conditions.

Chapter 20. Falling Interest Rate Structure and Capital Destruction

In Chapter 5 we pointed out that von Mises' concept of time preference is faulty. He says that there is a tendency for the time preference of every individual to converge to the same level. However, you cannot discipline Scrooge and the prodigal son so easily by brow-beating. You must have recourse to the Method of Marginalism to arrive at the right concept. You must pass from time preference to marginal time preference. If you do, then you have the floor below which the banks cannot push the rate of interest. Otherwise the marginal saver will withdraw gold from his bank account, thereby depleting bank reserves and forcing the bank to contract its outstanding credit. Time preference is more than just a pious wish. It has golden teeth, and it can bite.

Similarly, in Chapter 3 we pointed out that von Mises was not on firm grounds when he denied the existence of a connection between the rate of interest and the marginal productivity of capital. If the former increases, for example, the marginal producer will sell his material factor of production (or at least will stop maintaining it) and will buy the bonds of those producers whose productivity is higher. In this way a limit (ceiling) is set, above which the rate of interest cannot rise. It will have to stay between these two extremes, the floor and the ceiling, each of which must be studied separately in order to gain full understanding of the process of interest-rate formation. [*Ed. See figure 3B, 4 and 5 pp. 63 & 68*].

Two distinct arbitrage operations are involved. In case of the floor, it is the arbitrage of the marginal bondholder between the bond market and the gold market. In the case of the ceiling it is that of the marginal producer between the bond market and the market for capital goods. You cannot ignore either one, as von Mises tried to do. This is the reason that, before the synthesis brought about by research at NASoE, no theory of interest has succeeded to explain the phenomenon of interest satisfactorily.

Tragically, the failure of economists to provide an adequate theory of interest allowed governments and their central banks to disenfranchise people in locking them out from the process of the formation of interest rates. In particular, 'policymakers' pushed down the rate of interest to zero, depriving people and their pension funds of vital income. Mischief was done at both extremes. In the early 1980s we had "Volcker's course". Paul Volcker single-handedly pushed most of the American productive capital into submarginal territory. Interest rates were allowed to break away upwards in an effort to save the dollar from extinction. As they did, the marginal productivity of capital rose, causing wholesale capital destruction. Perfectly serviceable material factors of production were hauled to the scrap yard and pushed into oblivion. This meant nothing less than the deindustrialisation of America. As a consequence well-paying industrial jobs were exported wholesale to China and elsewhere.[43]

This episode of the early 1980's has never been satisfactorily explained. Mainstream Austrian economists remained silent. How could they speak up? They had no theory to guide them. The capital destruction was entirely pointless. The well-being of the American working man was sacrificed at the altar of the fetish: the irredeemable dollar. Having been laid off, American workers were forced to find low-paying jobs in the service sector. The American labour movement meekly accepted the atrocity without demur. Mainstream Austrian economists should have protested that *"Thou shalt not crucify American labour on this cross of paper money"*. [44]

Capital destruction was not confined to removing the ceiling of the range within which the rate of interest may move. Removing the floor from below the interest-rate structure was even worse, reinforced by the false propaganda- smokescreen of Keynesian economics that "low interest rates are good for you". They may have been good to bond speculators, banks included, but they were cruel to the American workers whose jobs were destroyed for good. The prolonged decline in the rate of interest (now in its fourth decade) was lethal. It resulted in the erosion, nay, in the wholesale destruction of capital. This process is not easy to understand because of the reluctance of the mind to admit that a continually falling interest-rate structure makes the financing of capital a losing proposition. It bankrupts perfectly viable firms forcing them to lay off their employees. Consistently falling interest rates make for deflation and, ultimately, for depression.[45]

Now we have a replay of 1933 when the ban on gold ownership herded the savings of the most conservative savers out of gold and into government bonds. A dramatic decline of the rate of interest and capital destruction followed as the only effective competitor of government bonds, gold was knocked out. Without exaggeration one may say that the Great Depression of the 1930's was the direct result of the hare-brained gold policies of President F. D. Roosevelt. We at NASoE were the first to point out that one of the most important roles of gold is to cordon off interest rates away from the black hole of zero interest that could gobble up the economy lock, stock, and barrel. Today the Fed is engineering zero interest using different means, but the outcome is still the same: wholesale capital destruction and snowballing unemployment.

Charlatans and saboteurs at the Fed would never admit that they are helpless. They pretend that it is they themselves who are pushing down interest rates under ZIRP (Zero Interest Rate Policy). When conditions improve, they say, the policy will be reversed. They pretend that they have the situation well in hand. They study the possible 'exit strategies' how to inch away from the black hole of zero interest in which they landed the world economy.

The truth is that they are scared. ZIRP did not work for Japan, rather, it contributed to the ruination of the most flourishing economy second only to that of the United States. It is now doing the same to America with a lag. Policymakers at the Fed have a 'conundrum' they cannot solve. They whistle in the dark and keep saying that the Fed can always generate inflation by revving up the printing presses. Open-ended money creation always brings about inflation, so they say. In reality, all it does is bring about more deflation, in the short run.

The Fed cannot see why open market operations, in particular Quantitative Easing, instead of creating more *inflation*, are bolstering *deflation*. Here is our solution to the conundrum. The Fed's open market purchases offer bond speculators risk-free profits galore. When they go on a bond-buying spree, it means that the new money created by the Fed is deflected. Instead of going into consumption or into commodity speculation, it goes into speculative bond purchases.[46] Thus it leads to a new round of fall in interest rates, stoking the fires of deflation. The ultimate result will be the complete devastation of the American and the world economy: wholesale capital destruction, domino-effect type bankruptcies, unprecedented unemployment. In one word: a replay the Great Depression of the 1930's, only made worse by the extremely weak and fast deteriorating international credit standing of the U.S. government.

The Fed has lost control. The car is careening into the ditch on the deflation-side of the road when the Fed wanted to steer it closer to the inflation-side. The steering mechanism has failed. Interest rates keep falling no matter what the Fed does. Capital destruction continues unabated. For more on the unintended consequences of the policy of open market operations of the Fed, see Appendix.

Addendum : How Falling Interest Rates Cause Capital Erosion

First I shall explain how bank capital is eroded, ultimately destroyed, by falling interest rates. Then I extend the reasoning to arbitrary firms.

We may assume that the entire capital of the bank is financed through the issuance of a bond b which is listed in the liability column of the balance sheet of the bank.

A "SEESAW EFFECT" operates between interest rates and bond prices: if the rate of interest falls, then bond prices go higher. and vice versa. The seesaw effect is recognised universally by all analysts and theorists. They realise that, at the prevailing lower rate of interest the fixed coupons of the bond b will be able to amortise the debt faster. That fact is reflected in the higher price the market is willing to pay for the bond b.

As a consequence, the LIQUIDATION VALUE of the bank goes up as well, because in case of liquidation the liability b must be covered. [47] The bond b must be bought back at a higher price than it had been sold earlier to raise capital. Thus there is a LOSS, that certainly shows up when the bank is liquidated. With proper accounting, however, which marks the balance sheet to market, there is no need to wait until the bank has to be liquidated. [48]The loss owing to the rise in liabilities will be recognised as soon as the next balance sheet is published. It inevitably shows up as an erosion of bank capital. Thus proper accounting may be seen as an EARLY WARNING SYSTEM for the banking business or, for that matter, any business using capital and has a balance sheet.[49]

However we look at it, the causality nexus from falling interest rates to capital erosion should be apparent. It must be taken into account. [50]

My 'Destruction of capital' argument (Part 1)

Suppose you issued bonds paying interest at 4% with no maturity date, for a total of $1,000,000. Your liability is $1,000,000. If the rate of interest is cut by half to 2% one day later, then your liability on the bond issue doubled: it is now $ 2,000,000 (because that is the capital you now need in order to generate the same income that $ 1 million generated yesterday). If you want to liquidate your liability, you have to come up with double of the proceeds of your bond issue for a loss of $1,000,000.

At any rate, the total loss to society is $1 million, which cannot be made to disappear by any argument, however clever!

Actually, it is even worse. Not only is there a loss on the new issue of shares but on the total capital of your enterprise as well. Half of your capital has been wiped out – along with the capital of every other firm, simultaneously, by the stroke of the pen. Everybody has to run twice as fast on the running belt just to stay abreast.

Incidentally, this is one of the main arguments to show the excellence of the gold standard. The gold standard may or may not be able to stabilise the price level, but it is most certainly able to stabilise the rate of interest! The scenario of interest rates being cut by half across the board simply cannot happen under a gold standard regime. It is inconceivable that a loss of capital be inflicted on all enterprises simultaneously.

The managers of fiat paper money put the muzzle on professors to conceal the fact that when they cut the rate of interest they actually inflicted a loss on the entire society, without exception. The professors are even made to sing the song of praise of monetary policy suggesting that lower interest rates are a blessing to business and to society. And how beautifully do they sing it! Incredibly, the public swallows the crap and, rather than invading the building of the Federal Reserve on Constitution Avenue in Washington, D.C. to throw the rascals out, they buckle down and slave on without saying as much as 'ouch'. They may complain about the weather, and about the higher price for bread, but won't complain about the conspiracy to which they have fallen victim.

Why do the professors meekly play the accomplice in this incredible fraud? Well, for one, they don't want to rock the boat. My argument exposes Keynes as a crank. 'The euthanasia of the rentier' is a thoroughly rotten slogan because it simply means the euthanasia of society through capital erosion and destruction. But it is at the same time a very successful slogan: it appeals to envy. The professors cannot bring themselves to admitting that their own university training, as well as the training they provide to the new generation, is the worst kind of deliberate brain poisoning in all history.

It has been well over a decade now since I have been preaching this in the classroom and on the internet. One or two in the audience applauded, but the rest just sat there shaking their heads. I believe it all boils down to the reluctance of the mind to admit that the rate of interest varies inversely with the bond price. This was the stumbling block for Keynes when he made the incredible blunder of asserting that there was a trade-off between inflation and unemployment.

We looked the effect of a single cut in the rate of interest, which is capital erosion. But what we have is a serial cut in the rate of interest, the effect of which is capital destruction across the board!

My 'Destruction of capital' argument (Part 2)

In Part One we have seen how the capital of financial firms is eroded (destroyed) under a falling interest-rate structure. We regarded the capital of a financial firm as a perpetual bond (consol). As the rate of interest is cut in half, the price of the consol doubles. It may look like a boon to the firm. But, alas, capital accounts must be listed in the liability column of the balance sheet, along with other debt, not in the asset column. As a result, cutting the interest rate in half results not in a gain but in a loss.

Essentially the same argument applies to producing firms as well. Since you have a lingering doubt about this applicability, so in this Part 2 I present a second argument coached in the language of production.

Widget is a company producing quality horseshoes (in the pre-automobile era). It has been paying dividends without interruptions for 100 years. It is clear that if it stopped paying dividends, then the production of horseshoes would come to a grinding halt. The stream of dividend payments, more precisely the value of the stream of dividend payments capitalised at the going rate of interest is the only valid measure of productive capital.

As we all know, Widget had to fold tent with the advent of the automobile age. We think we understand the reason. Widget's capital was destroyed as it was unable to produce a stream of dividends. The fact that its ability to produce horseshoes remained unimpaired did not matter a whit. People's thinking is conditioned that the only way the capital of a producing firm could be destroyed is through obsolescence.

But assume, for the sake of argument, that the Fed was established one hundred years earlier and its chairman, one Ben Bernanke, cut the going rate of interest from 4 to 2%. Of course, that did not the stop Widget's stream of dividends. Seemingly nothing much happened. If anything, a benefit was bestowed on society: it made the raising of new capital easier. But wait. Actually, something terrible has happened. Bernanke did something horribly destructive. He cut the capitalised value of Widget's stream of dividend payments in half. Because there was no change in the size of the actual dividends, this is not easy to see. What has changed was the rate at which the same stream of payment was capitalised. It was cut in half. As a result, the capital of Widget was cut in half by a stroke of Bernanke's pen, whether we like it or not.

We can understand the reluctance of the mind to admit that such an arbitrary erosion of capital values is possible by a stroke of the pen in the first place. And indeed, it would not have been possible under the gold standard. The inertia in the thinking of people makes them believe that if it was not possible in the 19th century, then it cannot be possible in the 21st. They think of the abolishing of the gold standard as just a minor house-keeping change that can have no effect on the foundation of the house. Yet, how wrong they are!

Widget's is not an isolated example. The same 50% erosion of capital hit all producing firms across the board. There would be no problem if all these firms could replace the missing part of their capital by new capital subscription. But it should be clear that only the most productive and most efficient firms could do that. The others are doomed.

It may take some time for the truth to sink in. Any adversity in the fortunes of Widget will hasten the day of reckoning. At one point in the future the creditors of Widget (who can read balance sheets) will call in their loans, forcing Widget to fold tent. It is inevitable. You could not fight the Principle of Causality. In physics, typically, the effect is instantaneous. In economics, the effect follows with a lag. Sometimes, with a lag of half a century.

The gold standard did not die a natural death. It was a victim of sabotage. The saboteurs were people in high places such as presidents, central bankers, Nobel-laureate economists, and the like, who had the power to stifle public debate of the underlying issues, such as the issue of destabilising the interest-rate structure, or the issue of opening the way to wholesale capital destruction. Why, they had the power to sidestep (nay, to trample on the Constitution).

The U.S. Constitution could not be clearer on the definition of the dollar in terms of the monetary metals, and the obligation of governments to meet their debt in specie. Today, the dollar is defined in terms of debt (actually, it is left completely undefined!), and the government retires its debt through juggling debts of different maturities. No matter: the enemies of peaceful and voluntary cooperation of people under the system of division of labour won't be stopped by trifles such as the Constitution, or by the threat of total destruction of capital across the board half a century later.

It is bad enough if the economy is hit with a one-time cut of its productive capital. But a saboteur named Bernanke introduced a system whereby the economy is hit serially. If allowed to continue, capital destruction ensues. The result is deflation, devaluation, depression.

My 'Destruction of capital' argument (Part 3).

In Part 2, I discussed the example of a 100 year old horseshoe factory, Widget, whose capital has been cut into half when Bernanke cut the rate of interest from 4 to 2%. You have challenged my logic in saying that, as long as Widget continues to pay dividends as before, capital erosion is a mere hallucination of my mind.

Well, let me continue my example in this Part 3. Another horseshoe factory, Gadget, was built in the meantime and, as it happened, the first batch of horseshoes were produced on the very same day Bernanke cut the rate of interest from 4 to 2%. We may assume that Gadget's quality of horseshoes, output and capacity are very similar to those of Widget. For book-keeping purposes Gadget has to put a value on its capital that it will enter it in its balance sheet. What will this value be? Why, it will be the value of its output capitalised at the prevailing interest rate of 2%. Therefore, following your logic, we conclude that the capital of Gadget is only about half of that of Widget.

But this is absurd! Widget is a 100 year old factory whose plant and equipment are worn and obsolete. They will soon have to be scrapped, whereas Gadget's plant and equipment are spanking new. When time comes for Widget to refurbish its plant and equipment and it applies for a loan (or floats a bond, or issues new shares), those who decide the merit of its loan application (or floating a bond, or issuing new shares) will not follow your logic. They will follow mine. The capital of Widget is not a penny greater than that of Gadget. If anything, it is smaller on account of its worn-out or obsolete plant and equipment, due to depreciation. Never mind that the capital of Widget was much higher yesterday. That's ancient history. It may be of interest to historians, but not to investors. On the day Bernanke cut the rate of interest in half, the capital of Widget (and that of all other producing firms as well) was also cut into half. If you say this is capricious, arbitrary and unjust, I agree. But that is how the market evaluates capital. Widget can put any fancy values on its capital in the balance sheet, it will impress nobody when it comes to selling the firm or financing the upgrading (or the acquisition of new) plant and equipment.

Up until World War II the Fed had a policy vehemently to deny that it was possible for a central bank to change the rate of interest along the yield curve arbitrarily and capriciously. The Fed admitted only that it had the ability and power to influence the very shortest of short interest rate, the so-called 'federal funds rate' at which member banks were lending and borrowing reserves overnight in order to square their books at the close of business. This policy was changed some time in the 1950's without much fanfare.

Today the policy is to let the public believe that the Fed has the power to change the rate of interest for any maturity simply by waving its magic wand any time at will.

It is easier to brow-beat people that way.

It is true that the Fed changing the federal funds rate has a ripple effect along the yield curve. But it is a far cry from cutting the rate interest in half, let alone doing it serially.

Chapter 21. The Theory of the Retail Trade

Retail trade encompasses the trade of first order (consumer) goods. The supply/demand equilibrium analysis does not provide a suitable setting for describing this trade. Adam Smith's real bills doctrine does. In particular, a spontaneous increase in the demand for consumer goods will not cause prices to rise. It will lead to an increase in bill circulation and, hence, to a fall in the discount rate. Supply will increase to match demand [51] through the mechanism of the discount rate. The low discount rate will enable some workers to quit the rank of wage earners and join the rank of self-employed businessmen. With very little capital they are able to bring an inventory to the consumers at attractive prices.

In chapter 9 we have seen how the dynamics of the retail trade can be described in terms of arbitrage between the market of first order goods and the bill market. Mainstream Austrian economics has missed this point in refusing to recognise the discount rate as independent from the rate of interest.

This was a major error of omission. Further refinement of the theory of the retail trade will show the interaction between the export-import trade and between the domestic and international bill markets.

Nowadays the world faces a huge problem: collapsing world trade repeating the experience of the great depression in the 1930's, when as a consequence of competitive devaluation of the pound sterling and the US dollar, world trade was engulfed in a trade war.

In view of our analysis of the retail trade we can see the root of the problem was, then as now, the failure of the victorious Entente powers to rehabilitate the international bill market. The theory of the gold standard was deplorably inadequate. It described the adjustment mechanism in terms of price-level changes in the surplus and deficit countries due to the change in the gold flow. We are consistent in our critique of the Quantity Theory of Money. Instead, we should describe the adjustment mechanism of the gold standard in terms of the Real Bills Doctrine.

Our theory refutes the supply/demand equilibrium theory in so far as the retail trade is concerned. An influx of gold into circulation need not cause rising prices of consumer goods. The new gold flows to the bill market bidding up bill prices, that is, pushing down the discount rate. The marginal shopkeeper responds by displaying new merchandise on his shelf. By the time the new gold percolates down to the consumer in the form of higher wages, the extra supply of consumer goods will be waiting for him on the shelves. Conversely, a gold outflow or gold hoarding will not necessarily cause falling prices. The gold is being withdrawn from the bill market, generating an extra supply of bills. This lowers bill prices, that is, it pushes up the discount rate. The marginal shopkeeper responds by eliminating merchandise from the shelf. In brief: supply smoothly adjusts itself to demand in the retail trade. There is no such thing as an autonomous change in the supply of consumer goods.

Appendix

Open Market Operations and Risk-free Bond Speculation

Risk-free speculation is like a long fuse. At the far end is the detonator that triggers enormously destructive forces – but only with a long lag after the fuse was lit at the other end. As more and more speculators climb on the bandwagon of undeserved free gifts, the economy plunges into an unsuspected back hole. The long fuse obscures the cause/effect nexus. In the post mortem the real cause of the disaster is hardly ever exposed and all kinds of false causes are proposed and blamed.

Government meddling in the economy is bad in any case and for many reasons. One of the reasons is that it may inadvertently give rise to risk-free speculation that will open up such a black hole. Politicians and civil servants have a rather limited intelligence. More often than not they are unable to grasp the delayed consequences of their own actions, as is the case with the nemesis of risk-free speculation. Nor is the perspicacity of academia much better. Economists often don't see further than the end of their nose, and fail to warn the powers-that-be of the unintended consequences of their inane action.

One instance of releasing the genie of risk-free speculation from the bottle was the illegal introduction of the policy of open market operations of the U.S. Federal Reserve System in the U.S. Treasury bond market in 1922. Illegal it certainly was: covering Federal Reserve credit with government debt was ruled out by the Federal Reserve Act of 1913. Eligible assets named in the Act were only two: gold and real bills. Government debt was specifically excluded. Steep and progressive penalties to pay were stipulated on offending Federal Reserve banks, to be levied by the U.S. Treasury. (As it turned out, this was tantamount to giving the fox the key to the chicken coop.) The consequence was the Great Depression of the 1930's, as I now proceed to show.

In 1922 the U.S. Federal Reserve officially introduced the terms "open market operations" and "open market policy" for a fundamentally new method of money creation and credit management. [52] It came hard on the heels of the spectacular collapse of the U.S. Treasury bond market in 1921. The crisis was covered up. The financial press hardly commented on it. Academia also thought that it was just a hiccup not worth a penetrating analysis. As a result of the 'hiccup' all American banks suffered a great loss of capital as they carried mostly government bonds on capital account. What could be safer? Bank officials looked at their own balance sheet incredulously. They had never thought such devastation was possible. They had believed that government paper was solid as the rock of Gibraltar. How could they in the future protect their capital against such a misfortune? They looked askance at the Federal Reserve.

The central bank had to do something in a hurry. It improvised. To pacify the bond market it announced an early version of 'Quantitative Easing' under a different name: they called it 'open market operations'. It was a revolution in central banking. Previously the central bank had a passive role to play. It let its clients take the initiative. The central bank's job was strictly passive: to post the rate at which its clients (commercial banks) might rediscount real bills in their portfolio if they chose to do so. Now the central bank started the lending process at its own initiative – rather than at that of the client. In buying and selling (mostly buying) U.S. government securities it turned from a passive to an active lender. The Fed buying Treasury bonds in the open market meant *lending to the U.S. Treasury.*

The illegal exercise was meant to be temporary at first. After the emergency was over the Federal Reserve intended to return to traditional central banking – and to legality. But the taste of the forbidden fruit was too good to give up. Open market operations, legal or otherwise, was quickly made a permanent fixture of central banking. Maybe Congress wouldn't notice the violation of the law (it didn't).

Through the stealthy introduction of open market operations the

Federal Reserve imperceptibly turned itself into a holding company of government bonds. The negative side effects of this radical departure from the traditional business model of central banking should have been considered at the time, but weren't. For one thing, the Federal Reserve has lost its ability to weather a crisis in which the liquidity of the central bank is of the foremost importance. Should both the Treasury and the Fed be in need of selling bonds, they would be find themselves in working at cross purposes. In such a case, of course, the Treasury would have the right of way. Good monetary policy would always be sacrificed on the altar of fiscal expediency. The list goes on and on.

But one negative side effect has, because of its enormity, eclipsed all others in importance. This was the fact that the open market operations of the central bank inevitably let the genie of bond speculation hitherto unknown, out of the bottle. And, as the speculators soon found out, bull speculation in government bonds was virtually risk-free as they could learn how to front-run the Fed (i.e. buy the bonds before the Fed had a chance to get to the ball.) In this way the speculators pocketed unearned profits at the expense of the public purse.

In 1952 Ludwig von Mises wrote an essay entitled *Monetary Reconstruction* as an epilogue to the English-language edition of his 1912 book *The Theory of Money and Credit*. A section of this essay describes a detailed plan to return the United States to the gold coin standard (from the international gold bullion standard as it prevailed in 1952). In this essay von Mises avoids the problem of the open market operations and its consequence, risk-free bond speculation, as well as the problem of the large holdings of government securities by the Fed. It should be clear that without addressing these problems no reform of the monetary system has a chance of success. His was an error of omission. Ever since mainstream Austrian economists ignore the problem altogether, and no penetrating analysis of open market operations is available, despite the urgent need. NASoE wants to fill that need. As a matter of fact, NASoE has identified the nexus between open market operations of the Fed and risk-free bond speculation.

Under the gold standard there was simply no bond speculation. The bond price was so stable that the small variations that might have occurred gave no occasion for profitable trading. Detractors of gold gleefully point to the possible swing of commodity prices under the gold standard. However, the gold standard is not ordained to stabilise commodity prices. Variations in prices are an important signal for producers as well as consumers. Rising prices prompt producers to increase production and consumers to contain consumption, and vice versa. Obeying these signals makes for shock-free operation of the economy. What the gold standard is ordained to do is to stabilise bond prices. That is tantamount to saying that the gold standard is ordained to stabilise the rate of interest. History convincingly shows that the gold standard has been eminently successful in doing it.

Until, that is, the unveiling of the policy of open market operations heralded a sea change in 1922. The harmonious system whereby the gold standard stabilised the interest-rate structure was all of a sudden shattered by the stampede of bond speculators. The central bank unwittingly served as a sort of Santa Claus in providing the necessary cash for reckless bond speculation (incidentally allowing the banks to participate in the bonanza) – to use the apt simile of Melchior Palyi. Of course, speculators knew that open market operations on a net basis would always be open market purchases, hardly ever sales. Open market sales were for window dressing only. Why, open market sales of government securities on a net basis would be tantamount to (heaven forbid!) contracting Federal Reserve credit. Monetary policy was turned into a great opportunity for speculators to pre-empt the central bank in buying the bonds first, in order to dump them into the lap of the same central bank at a higher price afterwards. Speculators knew that the central bank must make periodic trips to the open market to purchase its quota of bonds in order (1) periodically to increase the money supply, or (2) to provide a prop to the sagging market for government bonds. Speculators were on watch. They forestalled the central bank, forcing it to shell out far more money than the going price for bonds. The loss was borne by the general public. Speculators knew exactly how to front-run the Fed. This type of activity is their trade mark. As far as the speculators were concerned, there was virtually no risk involved. It was the perfect crime. Bond monetisation (specifically disallowed by the Federal Reserve Act of 1913) was not a godsend. There was a price to pay: it was followed by an upward move in the cost structure for the global economy. Shrinking profit margins were imposed on all enterprises. The result was job cuts, reduced budgets for expansion of producing activity and even neglect of capital maintenance.

To illustrate the unconscionable profits made possible by the open market operations of the Fed, consider the fact that bond prices have doubled three times since 1981 and in the 21st century continued to double again several times. This makes the market for U.S. government debt one of the longest-lived bull markets on record.

In 1980 it took a decade for the bond prices to double. But since the Great Financial Crisis burst upon the scene, the pace has appeared to have accelerated. Between 1980 and 1990 long-term interest rates fell from 16 to 8 percent. This triggered the first doubling of bond prices. Between 1990 and 2000 interest rates fell further from 8 to 4 percent. This triggered the second. By 2008 as interest rates fell from 4 to 2 percent. This triggered the third doubling of the bond prices. All in all, the bond price increased eight-fold in 27 years (!). It had a tremendous effect on the speculative spirit. The bull market in bonds afforded fabulous profits, all virtually risk free, to the bond speculators. This aspect of the interest saga is completely ignored by economists, the Austrian mainstream included.

Something noteworthy happened in 2008 that changed the picture. It was the political wrangle about increasing the debt-limit of the U.S. government. Republicans gained a majority in the House of Representatives (where all spending bills must originate). They refused to play ball with the Democrats. This stopped the fall in interest rates temporarily. Speculators withheld their bond purchases waiting to see which way the cat would jump. Public discussion about alternatives to the U.S. Congress' telltale ritual of periodically increasing the debt limit on the government debt started. "Repeal it!" cried Federal Reserve Chairman Greenspan, by then out of office.

Observers gleefully declared that the "bond bubble has been pricked". They expected a huge jump in interest rates and a corresponding collapse of bond prices. How wrong they were! When the political wrangling ended and the debt limit was duly raised, interest rates started falling again from 2 percent. It appeared that bond prices were going to double again. Observers were flabbergasted. What happened?

Well, bond speculators hesitated a bit but as soon as the dust settled they decided that 'happy times are here again'. They started buying the bonds again for the risk-free profits that the raising of the debt ceiling afforded. Nobody pointed out that this guaranteed the continuation of deflation.

As of the New Year of 2013, the touch-and-go nature of the bull market in bonds continues. New catchwords such as "operation twist" and "fiscal cliff" were invented to camouflage illegal or semi-legal practices. Operation twist refers to the Fed's selling T-bills from portfolio replacing them with T-bonds. It is a shameless manoeuvre of borrowing short to lend long, threatening the yield curve with inversion.

To summarise, open market operations (read: purchases) of the central bank is not only illegal (in the United States) but it is also destructive as the falling interest rate structure it engenders, creates massive destruction of capital indiscriminately, through the mechanism that connects falling interest rates to rising bond prices.

Relentlessly rising bond prices destroy capital in the producer sector. This can be seen through the fact that producers must compete with bond speculators. They are squeezed to redeploy their capital in the bond market if their revenues are no match for the profits of bond speculators. The financial institutions, including the banks are particularly hard hit by the earthquake destroying capital. They must carry government bonds on capital account by law. As the price of government bonds rise, their capital accounts are undermined

(since capital is a liability of the bank that belongs to its shareholders!)

The dollar may not be beyond repair and Trump may be the one to repair it.

Introduction

The dollar is a through and through debauched currency as shown by the fact that in less than one hundred years it has lost 97 percent of its purchasing power. This may be a record in the history of decaying and moribund currencies that have managed to survive as long as a century. The debauchery was deliberately fomented at the behest of the federal government even at the expense of overthrowing the Constitutional monetary order of the Republic. In what follows I shall enumerate four étapes of this fomentation.

(1) The default on the government's domestic gold obligations (including the unconstitutional and highly repulsive, not to use the Biblical term “abominable” (Proverbs, XX-10) confiscation of the gold coins of the citizenry, pursuant to an executive order of F.D. Roosevelt (a democrat) in March, 1933, just a few days after his inauguration as president.

(2) The default on the government's international gold obligations (including gold embargo that apparently is still in force as witnessed by the recent refusal to release Germany's gold pursuant to an executive order of R.M. Nixon (a republican) on August 15, 1971.

(3) Lesser known is the violation of the F.R. Act of 1913 (before amendments) which explicitly forbids the construction of F.R. credit on government debt with stiff and progressive penalties for non-compliance that was the result of a conspiracy between the U.S. Treasury and the F.R. System that started in 1922 to initiate open market operation of the Federal Reserve banks. As a side effect bond speculators are invited to reap risk-free profits by front-running the Fed (buying the bonds beforehand to drop them later in the lap of the latter at elevated prices). The policy of open market operation is

the main tool in the hand of the government to suppress the rate of interest, in some cases all the way to zero.

Thus are the savings of the people syphoned off surreptitiously. Moreover, capital is being destroyed unobserved. In more details: falling interest rates are tantamount to rising bond prices that increase the liability of banks and other firms on capital account. Any unintentional addition to the liability column of the balance sheet means capital destruction.

All the dollars that were created after 1922 have come about through check-kiting.In more details, the Treasury and the Fed have exchanged liabilities allowing more liabilities to be created without limits.The situation is this: F.R. notes are backed by U.S. Treasury bonds payable in the selfsame F.R. notes for which they serve as collateral. The result is the building of a Babylonian tower of liabilities for which nobody takes responsibility.

(4) More recent is the violation of Contract Law allowing the replacement of physical gold by digital gold (a.k.a. "gold in the clouds") The physical gold was then hypothecated, swapped for paper gold, sold, and spirited out of the country illegally.

As a result of this prestidigitation, it is doubtful that the American gold reserve is intact. Some say the U.S. may not have any physical gold left. President Trump, should he decide to initiate the rehabilitation of the Gold Standard Act of 1900 that was sabotaged by Roosevelt in 1933, might find Fort Knox utterly empty and be forced to abort the initiative for reasons of the lack of an adequate gold reserve.

The purpose of this article is to draw attention to the saving grace, namely, to a freak incident that may make it possible for Trump to reclaim the American gold reserve and go ahead with his initiative.

While he was trying to bury the gold standard, Roosevelt ordered the confiscated gold coins of the citizenry be melted down – an outrageously destructive act known as the Great Coin Melt. As we shall see, the measure back-fired. Here is the fortuitous fact that makes the finding of the hypothecated and exported American gold reserve easy. Roosevelt had the confiscated gold recast in bar form (400oz. or 12,5kg "international good delivery bars"). Not a single other country followed the American lead in melting down its gold coinage.

Indelible watermark

The obvious intent behind Roosevelt's Great Coin Melt was to prevent any future Administration from reversing the unconstitutional measures of the Roosevelt Administration. In and of itself this was a highly anti-democratic and immoral act. No Administration should have the power to commit all future Administration to continue its own pet policies. Periodic elections are held in democratic countries precisely in order to give a chance to the electorate to reject objectionable policies.

Because in 1933 the American gold reserve encompassed virtually all the monetary gold in the world, it is apparent that Roosevelt went all out in his zeal to expunge the gold standard from the face of the world.

Now we see that this effort was frustrated because of an oversight in the execution of the Great Coin Melt.

The American gold coinage did not consist of 999 fine gold. It was an alloy of only 925 fine; the rest being copper in order to make the coins harder and more resistant to wear and tear. Consequently the "international good delivery bars" into which they had been cast before they were hypothecated, sold and spirited out of the country, all carry an indelible "watermark": the impaired substandard fineness. This betrays their origin as having come from the American gold reserve.

The upshot is that the Trump Administration will not be thwarted if it wants to rehabilitate the Gold Standard Act of 1900, as plotted by Roosevelt. American monetary gold that has been illegally hypothecated and spirited out of the country can be tracked down. All President Trump has to do is to declare "watermarked" gold contraband

and claim it as gold that is still part of the American gold reserve, wherever it may be located and whoever may be its putative owner.

There's no need to repatriate the gold by force. As pointed out, contraband gold carries an indelible "watermark".

Having "tabooed" contraband gold, President Trump will promote the U.S. as the country with the largest gold reserve of any country in the world, beating China and Russia to it, two countries which scramble to achieve that desirable goal.

Moreover, the United States under the Trump Administration will be able to reverse the worrisome flow of gold from the Occident to the Orient that has bled the Western countries white, making them virtually impotent economically and financially.

The repercussions are truly breath-taking. The U.S. government debt and the dollar can convincingly be made gold-redeemable once again. American Treasury paper will shine, recapturing its former glory as the most desirable asset second only to gold itself to own by anyone, anywhere, anytime. The illegal check-kiting between the U.S. Treasury and the Fed can be terminated immediately.

Moreover, the United States under the Trump Administration will be able to reverse the worrisome flow of gold from the Occident to the Orient that has bled the Western countries white, making them virtually impotent economically and financially. The output of the world's gold mines will flow to the U.S. Mint rather than to China and Russia.

The Bric-countries and a China-Russia coalition can no longer bully the United States threatening to dump the dollar as the world's reserve currency, unless they are prepared to make their currency gold redeemable. That they won't be able to do if only because their gold reserves are insufficient (at least for the time being). The same applies to the so-called "nuclear option" (namely, the potential blackmail of China to dump U.S. Treasury bonds in order to cause financial turmoil to the discomfiture and detriment of the U.S.

Lacking moral courage

Keynesian politicians could have initiated an amendment to make the irredeemable dollar conform to the Constitution. They never had the moral courage to do so.

A Constitutional monetary system could never be built on a debt-based currency. The reason is that there is no way to define the monetary unit in a way that is logically sufficient.

In more details: if we define it as debt, then, we have to be able to say whose debt it is. This leads to a vicious circle. Assume it is the debt of A, represented by the bond a. Then a is in the liability column of the balance sheet of A. Let the liability be balanced by the bond b issued by B. Then b is a liability of B. Supposed it is balanced by the bond c issued by C. And so on and so forth. We have an infinite chain meaning that the currency has no backing whatsoever; it is nobody's liability. This being the case, it can scarcely have any value. The "experts" chime in saying that as a matter of fact the chain is finite and its last link is x, the bond issued by X, the U.S. Treasury. The circumstance that X is the world's greatest debtor with a debt that keeps growing day in and day out, and that X has neither the intention nor the means ever to retire its debt is conveniently sidestepped. Once again the "experts" chime in suggesting that there is no need to retire the debt of X because x is acceptable as the ultimate extinguisher of debt.

The truth is, however, that there is only one ultimate extinguisher of debt, gold, the peerless asset that has no counterpart in the liability column of the balance sheet of any other economic unit.

Opening the Mint to Gold

There is some urgency that the Trump Administration act quickly and expeditiously to make the dollar gold-redeemable again through reclaiming the hypothecated American gold reserve on foreign soil.

By the same token, equally important is that the Trump Administration open the U.S. Mint forthwith to the unlimited coinage of gold free of seigniorage charges (as distinct from assay charges), that was forcibly and unconstitutionally closed by Roosevelt in 1933. This will invite the world's gold mines to bring forth their surplus gold and exchange it to spanking shiny American gold coinage, ounce for ounce, in unlimited quantity – preferably before China and Russia wake up and open theirs in an effort to thwart the U.S. One should see this as the real danger threatening the U.S. If there ever was a "nuclear option" then that's it: China and Russia opening their Mints to gold before the U.S. does.

Once the word is out that the Trump Administration is studying the matter of rehabilitating the Gold Standard Act of 1900, everybody will try to second-guess what the new gold price will be as quoted in the irredeemable F.R. notes.

As it turns out, it does not matter. The issue will not be determined on Quantity Theory of Money considerations. The number of gold coins to be struck will not be decided by the U.S. Treasury, nor by the Federal Reserve. The new gold price will not be fixed by the government: it will be fixed by the public at large. This exactly as it was envisaged by the Founding Fathers when they drafted the U.S. Constitution. They did not want the government to decide such a momentous matter as the size of the stock of money in circulation. Significantly, the Constitution did not establish a central bank for the country. Instead, it established the U.S. Mint, thus conferring the right to 'create' money [53] on the public at large.

It is not widely recognised that the American banking system is insolvent and is close to the point of declaring bankruptcy. The same is true for the most important banks abroad as well.[54] The Trump Administration in putting the dollar on a gold basis will avert a devastating international banking crisis and should earn the gratitude and admiration of the world for its foresight and courage.

To recapitulate, when all is said and done the truth is revealed that no irredeemable currency can ever play the role of the ultimate extinguisher of debt. In paying down debt with irredeemable currency debt is merely shifted from one bank to another (ultimately, to the

U. S. Treasury), or from one debtor to another. But shifting debt is not the same as extinguishing it. The only ultimate extinguisher of debt that exists in our world is gold, because as an asset it never occurs in the liability column of the balance sheet of a counter-party. This is why under the regime of irredeemable currency debt can only grow, never decline, imparting great instability to the financial system. By contrast, under a gold standard total debt is kept in check because the rate of interest acts as an obstruction to credit expansion.

The rehabilitation of the wage fund

It is not true that the gold standard is contractionist, deflation-prone, and government spending and unbalanced budgets are needed to keep the wheels of the economy spinning and to keep workers at their jobs – as charged by the Keynesians.

Rather than causing unemployment, the gold standard alone makes it possible through the market in real bills to create the Wage Fund out of which the wages of workers could be paid, if need be, a quarter (3 months, 13 weeks, 91 days) before the sale of merchandise to the ultimate consumer.

The horrendous tsunami of unemployment that engulfed the world economy in the 1930's was not caused by the gold standard. It was caused by the victorious Entente powers not reopening the London market in real bills after the cessation of hostilities in 1918. As is well-known, prior to 1913 the production and distribution of consumer goods was financed by real bills drawn on London maturing in gold. The destruction of the Wage Fund was the consequence of that decision. In the absence of a market in real bills there was no one to advance the wages of the workers. They had to be laid off.

The victorious Entente powers were motivated by their neurotic fear of German efficiency. They could no longer blockade the country, so they blocked its bills financing exports and imports.

The destruction of the Wage Fund and the horrendous unemployment in its wake was predicted by the German economist Heinrich

Rittershausen. Unfortunately, his warning was dismissed as chauvinistic German propaganda. Another German economist, Wilhelm Röpke said that it was not the gold standard that failed but those on whose care it was entrusted.

The threat of unemployment is still with us. We still lack a Wage Fund.

President Trump could remove the threat of unemployment for once and all. He could recreate the Wage Fund. To do this he would allow the trade of real bills drawn on New York, maturing in gold. After a century of hiatus, this measure would work miracles. Competitive devaluation of currencies ("race to the bottom")would come to an end. The threat of trade war would vanish.

How realistic is this scenario ?

Well, just as realistic as it was to expect that Donald Trump would beat Hillary Clinton in the last presidential election. Yet it happened. Very soon Trump will be confronted with the dollar problem and the problem of proliferating debt the country faces. No one can offer a credible solution. President Trump's economic advisors, Judy Shelton, Alan Greenspan, Ben Bernanke must tell him that the only way to rein in runaway debt is to bring gold, the only and trusted ultimate extinguisher of debt back into the international monetary system.

The picture is ugly. Trump has to choose between two destructive outcomes: inflation and deflation. The latter means allowing debt reduction to proceed through bankruptcies; the former means debt reduction to proceed through debasing the dollar to the point of worthlessness. It is quite likely that incumbent Treasury and Fed officials will push him to opt for the former. This is what their policies since the turn of the century and millennium suggests. There is no memory in this country of a Zimbabwe-style inflation. The American people will not stand for it. That's not why they sent Donald Trump to the White House.

Trump must realise that if the destructive gold policy of Roosevelt's first monetary revolution is followed, eighty-five years later, by a second, with his constructive gold policy, then deflation and inflation can be averted. He has the power to pull it off. Has he got the intelligence?

The alternative is that the U.S. dollar goes the way of the Zimbabwe dollar.

Trump must remember that although Napoleon's Empire is long gone, yet its currency, also called Napoleon (the 20 franc gold coin) still lives and prospers two hundred years later.

Can President Trump hope to make the dollar match that record?

If he repairs it, maybe.

December, 2016.

Notes

[Endnotes by Peter Van Coppenolle.]

[1] Professor Fekete won a.o. the *International Currency Essay Contest* sponsored by Bank Lips in 1996, with his entry called Whither Gold? after he published a breakthrough article 'Towards a Dynamic Microeconomics' in Laissez-Faire magazine of 1996.

[2] See Dr. G. Campagnolo, *Criticisms of Classical Political Economy, Menger, Austrian economics and the German Historical School*, Routledge, London, 2010. pp 286-287. According to Mengers' notes and correspondence, he distanced himself of mathematical versions such as Walras's version of marginal utility and a fortiori Gossen's, who seemed to have suffered from delusional visions of grandeur, besides having based his subjectivism on shaky grounds.

[3] The term seems attributed for the first time to Anthonie Destutt de Tracy (1754 – 1836), a French advisor of Napoleon, who supported the need for a system of ideas that could be the basis for a 'rational' and just society. De Tracy fell out of Imperial favour and Napoleon called de Tracy an "ideologue": a thinker with a muddled metaphysics of benefit to no one ...

[4] See Eric Voegelin, *The New Science of Politics, An Introduction*, University of Chicago Press, 1987, pp. 52-75. Eric Voegelin separates the lovers of wisdom (φιλοσοφοι - philosophoi) from the lovers of opinion (φιλοδοξα - philodoxa). The former word has survived until today. The latter word did not. Eric Voegelin replaces the term *philodoxa* with 'intellectual', to differentiate the person from the philosopher.

[5] M. Latzer, S.W. Schmitz (ed.) *Carl Menger and the Evolution of Payment Systems: From Barter to Electronic Money*, Edward Elger Pub., 2002, 191 p. The first part of this book contains Carl Menger's original article on money.

[6] L. von Mises, *Human Action A Treatise on Economics*, LVMI, Auburn, Alabama 1998, reprint 1st. edition, p. 395 et seq. and p. 468, Ch. 19 – The Gold Standard, p. 468 et seq. See also International Monetary Cooperation, p. 473-475.

[7] 'Positive' here means 'the opposite of negative' and has not the meaning of positivistic such as the 'positing' or the 'laying down' of the law as it is, 'because we say so.'

[8] I.e. by reducing its purchasing power in reality whilst all the way denying wrongdoing, by hiding behind a nominalism law as a fig leaf, manufactured by academics, where 'inflation' is presented as 'natural'. Nothing can be done about it ... Which is more of an insult to people's intelligence than an explanation.

[9] L. von Mises, supra, p. 441.

[10] M. Latzer, S.W. Schmitz (ed., supra,) contains Carl Menger's article on the genesis of money.

[11] Dr. Prof. Heinrich Rittershausen, *Unemployment as a Problem of Turnover Credits and the Supply of Means of Payments*, Jena Verlag, 1930. Translated into English by an unknown source. The original German text is still available.

[12] To be fair: the German term "*Arbeitsleistung*" may be translated to the modern term "energy"; Karl Marx used the term "*Arbeitskraft*" which translates to "labourer." In this instance, the German language (*Arbeit*) has more symbols (words) with finer and more differentiated meaning than English (labour). Menger never subscribed to the 'labour theory of value'.

[13] Marx reduced the human person to a class and his actions to a class phenomenon. Marx states for instance that '...all wars were always class wars'. Surely, the Peloponnesian war wasn't? Nor was the Persian war ? Marx continues and turns his facile pamphlet prose into a religion displaying all the characteristics of Auguste Comte's approach, the father of positivism. One does not question certain dogmas, so be a good socialist. Like Comte's Church of Positivism, in a Marxist system, the State is the Church, the scientists are its priests. See for a penetrating study: Eric Voegelin *From Enlightenment to Revolution*, Duke University Press, Durham, 1975.

[14] Gold and silver both enjoy, as they always did, very slowly declining marginal utility functions, which makes it 'nature-given' instead of manufactured by man, such as all fiat currencies. The latter do not enjoy such a slowly declining marginal utility. The evidence here is overwhelming by simply looking at a chart of the gold 'price' in fiat terms like the US$. If the marginal utility of the US$ were constant, than the gold chart would show a persistent, relentless and unrecoverable decline against this constant, showing its inferior marginal utility to the US$. The opposite is true! This is proof positive that a nature-given cannot ever be repealed by man. The (nearly) constant marginal utility of gold is not man made; it is 'nature-given' in the sense that it is an uncoordinated spontaneously happening event that persist over the ages. Small chance the any of

this will ever be taught at any level of any school.

[15] Without turning the people behind the market process, responsible for the bid/ask spread, into any sort of object. 'The market' is still a process involving economising people; it is not an object, nor a glorified unquestionable dogmatic fetish. Market processes take place because people need exchanges in a manifold of ways to satisfy just as many needs.

[16] L. von Mises, supra, p.86.

[17] The Logos (λογοσ) and the Nous (νους) are concepts discussed in Heraclitus and Plato respectively, meaning literally the Word and the Mind. The noösphere is the sphere occupied by consciousness; the logosphere is the concept that Heraclitus used for the same. A similar concept of the noösphere was reintroduced by the Jesuit philosopher (and millenarian transhumanist) P. Teilhard de Chardin (1881 – 1955) in 1922 as well as the Soviet mineralogist Vladimir Vernadsky (1863 – 1945) in 1936.

[18] I am making abstraction of other issues such as marketing advantages etc. Although the 'price' of a product is only one dimension, in a falling interest rate structure, the WACC or Weighted Average Cost of Capital drops, making itself felt not only in product pricing, but also in the financing of marketing costs, etc.

[19] For an actual example of such policy proposal, see W. Buiter, "Negative Nominal Interest Rates: Three Ways to Overcome the Lower Zero Bound," NBER Working paper 15118, June 2008.

[20] Erosion of equipment means off course a depreciation (wear and tear) due to its normal use or due to extraordinary circumstances, the latter forcing capital equipment into early retirement.

[21] A 'quadrillion dollar' in this instance is no indication of value; it is simply a number. A 'dollar' is just a name or label in the positivist legal and nominalist sense of the word. The sentence becomes meaningless if interpreted as a mass of value, for it cannot measure anything.

[22] L. von Mises, *Human Action*, supra, Chapter XIX, p.521.

[23] For the meaning of 'reason' and 'teleology' see Aristotle *Nicomachean Ethics*. 'Reason' for Hellenic thinkers did not exclude the metaphysical, e.g. to question the gods or God was seen as 'unreasonable.' We read this in Aeschylos' Prometheus where Prometheus, being fettered to a rock, shouts that he 'hates the gods.' Observe Hermes' answer to Prometheus ... Teleology as seen by Plato or

Aristotle means that the highest good in this life to be obtained by any reasonable, prudent (*phronesis*) and intelligent man (*spoudaios*) is the *bios theoretikos* or the contemplative live (in Aristotle) or the political life (in Plato.) In short: human lives are principally ordered by the existence of the gods (or God). We all live *sub specie mortis* and we had better live exemplary lives.

[24] There may exist several attenuating circumstances. Von Mises had to live through two world wars. He feared for his life and became a German exile in isolation in the United States. By then, nobody would blame him for losing some of his energy. I do not blame him of gross wilful failure or criminal negligence. I am stating that for whatever reason - and von Mises had already been exemplary in Vienna- it is incumbent on the next generation of scholars to come up with improvements. NASoE purports to do just that.

[25] P. Van Coppenolle, *The Austrian Business Cycle Revisited,* Brussels, 2012. ISBN 5800094365307.

[26] Economic activity of the entrepreneur.

[27] L. von Mises was a brilliant academic, but it was Menger who observed daily markets in his early career as financial journalist. He had a front row seat to watch the Vienna stock exchange crash in 1873, the establishment of the Austro-Hungarian Imperial Reserve Bank in 1860, housed next to the Vienna Stock Exchange. Menger lived during the reign of the Latin Monetary Union, to which Austria-Hungary subscribed and which Menger defended in a parliamentary commission (1892).

[28] Virgil, *Aeneid,* III, 57.

[29] Anyone visiting a previously Communist Bloc country, knew that people as well as privileges could be obtained with cigarettes, jeans, nylons. The same is visible everywhere in prisons, where drugs and cell phones circulate fast and furiously.

[30] Both gold and silver were hoarded.

[31] Please note that 'modern' money forms like cyber-money in all its variants, was born from a revolt against *quantity* of government issued money. Gold on the other hand is not scarce; with a 50 to 80 year stocks-to-flow ratio, it is abundant. Cyber money may succeed or fail; it needs 'marketability' or what is the same: currency and needs to beat the marketability of all other goods. I.e. *quality.*

[32] See note 13 above.

[33] 'Debt' means financial debt and not the moral duty to return some-

thing borrowed. Also, most legal systems provide for the case when a goods transaction cannot take place due to the destruction of the good. Instead, a sum of money needs to be handed over in redemption. Debt in a general sense can be settled in many ways, always to the satisfaction of the creditor. To preclude abuse, debts are converted to financial debts, i.e. amounts that can be certain or that are ascertainable, insofar and inasmuch as it is possible to do so when needed. Obviously, the damages for the death of a person are not really ascertainable, so they have to be imposed by a legal ruling. I.e. a person is not a 'good' with a value, although a person's life has value. The damage can never be compensated with money. However, a monetary amount will be granted as damages, lest one reverts to a legal system based on blood feud, calling an eye for an eye.

[34] Triffin's dilemma or paradox : the country whose currency foreign nations wish to hold (the global reserve currency) must be willing to supply the world with an extra supply of its currency to fulfil world demand for this 'reserve' currency and thus cause a trade deficit, a.k.a. sovereign debt.

[35] See what happens to normal mortals when they try to cover one check by issuing another one.

[36] This principle is not a legal one, but a metaphysical or moral one. The government as law giver exempts itself from its own laws by writing out a law. Which is in essence the same as getting a note from your parents exempting you from swimming classes. As if the 'sovereign will' of the 'sovereign people' will engage in check-kiting for the fun of lying to themselves.

[37] The observant reader will of course remember Plato, describing in his Republic, what a statesman should be like ... Or Aristotle describing the virtues of the spoudaios.

[38] Adam Smith, *An inquiry into the Nature and causes of the Wealth of Nations*, 1776, Book II, Ch.2. "Of Money considered as a particular Branch of the general Stock of Society, or of the Experience of maintaining the National Capital", p. 174. (depending on print):

> *"The gold and silver money which circulates in any country may very properly be compared to a highway, which, while it circulates and carries to market all the grass and corn of the country, produces itself not a single pile of either. The judicious operations of banking, by providing, if I may be allowed so violent a metaphor, a sort of waggon-way through the air, enable the country to convert, as it were, a great part of its highways into good pastures and corn-fields, and thereby to increase very considerably the annual produce of its land and labour. The commerce and indus-*

try of the country, however, it must be acknowledged, though they may be somewhat augmented, cannot be altogether so secure when they are thus, as it were, suspended upon the Daedalian wings of paper money as when they travel about upon the solid ground of gold and silver."

[39] It is clear that even Menger, like Aristotle or Plato, would not endorse indiscriminate licentious personal freedom at any cost. That is why the ancients like Aristotle do not hand down a 'book of rules'. The spoudaios knows through the psyche, his conscience, what right order is and applies this fixed justice principle into action in the ever changing world. Personal morals and larger ethics find their source in the eternal law, but only come to fruition in human action. For a penetrating analysis, see Eric Voegelin *Plato and Aristotle,* Collected Works Vol. 16, Order and History Vol III, University of Missouri Press, 2000. (ed. Dante Germino). Also: Edward Feser, Self-Ownership and the rights of children: towards a more conservative libertarianism, Journal of Libertarian Studies, 2004, comes to the same conclusion.

[40] This book was in the possession of Ludwig von Mises and of Carl Menger. The latter's library is currently in Japan. Menger bequeathed his library, and he was a keen bibliophile, to his (common law) wife Hermine, who sold it to the highest bidder during the difficult interwar years. Menger's library is kept at the Centre for Historical Social Science Literature (CHSSL), Hitotsubashi University, Tokyo, Japan.

[41] That is the present value (PV) or market price of the bond (currently).

[42] Remember that a positive and unhindered rate of interest is the brake on unlimited demand for gold.

[43] Note that in older times, but before Communism took over China, international trade was quite open, but jobs **never left home** for China ...

[44] A reference to William Jennings Bryan, a United States Representative of Nebraska. He vehemently opposed the silver demonetisation – the crime of the century – of 1872-1873.

[45] A relentlessly falling interest rate structure would not necessarily affect an entrepreneur's balance sheet, but his income statement will suffer, due to the relative high cost of financing (in retrospect) that reduce profitability.

[46] The public is told that this newly created money will 'trickle down.' The truth is: it was never more difficult for a private person to bor-

row from a bank. Literally trillions of dollars, euro's and yen's have been created, but they do not show up in people's wallets at all. They sit on bank books, who's back-office traders do what they are best in: pre-empt the Fed and earn themselves a (large) bonus.

[47] Under a gold standard, interest rates fluctuate between floor and ceiling and the entire range is comparatively small and manageable. (fig. 4) A mildly rising rate would be reflected by a mild downward revision of both assets and liabilities. Conversely, a mildly dropping interest rate would be reflected by a mildly rising asset and liability valuation. But under fiat conditions - and interest rates are not under control of the Fed- the ceiling rate of interest is controlled by the productivity rate of the marginal capital (bond) speculator and the floor rate is determined by the liquidity preference (instead of time preference) of the marginal speculator. (Fig. 5)

[48] Due to the legally imposed accounting assumption of a 'continuation of business as usual, that is under normal circumstances,' liabilities are prevented from revaluation upwards. That is, under this assumption of normal continuation, the bond issuer pays out as per the agreed schedule without need to revalue at the market price i.e. the liquidation value or the present value. Only once a business applies for bankruptcy or for some legal protection against creditors, may the assumption be challenged and set aside. The revaluation upward to the liquidation value or present value. of outstanding debt comes at the expense of the current Profit and Loss account, obviously reducing profits. Although perfectly legitimate economic reasons exists to readjust the balance sheet and profit and loss statement, this readjustment almost certainly will provoke an unpleasant reaction from fiscal authorities, who see 'their' income slashed by this readjustment.

[49] But as seen in note 48, fiscal authorities dislike such revaluation at 'their' expense.

[50] This was taken up in an unpublished fiscal LLM thesis by Peter Van Coppenolle at Tilburg/Leuven University, 2010. Fiscal Profit Determination with a Focus on Capital Gains and Inflation taxation across the Benelux Countries and Switzerland.

[51] See Say's law.

[52] See: *Open Market Policy and Totalitarian Control* by Melchior Palyi, "The Review of Politics", vol. I., no. 3, pp 320-332, July, 1939.

[53] 'Create money' means striking coins from old or new gold. The creation is obviously not *ad libitum* by any central authority, but en-

tirely at the discretion of any gold owner.

[54] No amount of Basel *n* regulations nor any strictness of liquidity tests will avoid the bankruptcy of all fiat banks, for reasons that have everything to do with the sidestepping of the "end of the chain" issue. Remarkably, this 'final cause' issue has been known since Plato and Aristotle (at the very least), repeated by Aquinas and others. The very fact of central bankers managing to sidestep Aristotle, Plato and Aquinas and everyone else with the 'finality' question in mind, bears witness to either the unwillingness to recognise the issue – perhaps by thwarting the whistleblowers – or to a seriously pathological situation in the educational systems of the world. In short : governments – in the so-called West – are divorced from the Church of Religion, but have overtly kept a mistress: that other significant woman is called the Church of Science, who was found to be more compliant and willing. See Rupert Sheldrake *The Science of Delusion*.

Index of Names

Index of Subjects

www.ingramcontent.com/pod-product-compliance
Lightning Source LLC
Chambersburg PA
CBHW041305210926
51851CB00006B/13/J
9789082065527